CHEAT IT ALL

CHEAT IT ALL

A YOUNG-EATER'S GUIDE TO GOOD FOOD AND MORE

VEDANT BAHRI

Photography

PUJA BAHRI

ANSHIKA VARMA

Food Styling

PUJA BAHRI

NIYOGI
BOOKS

Published by

NIYOGI BOOKS

D-78, Okhla Industrial Area, Phase-I
New Delhi-110 020, INDIA
Tel: 91-11-26816301, 49327000
Fax: 91-11-26810483, 26813830
email: niyogibooks@gmail.com
website: www.niyogibooksindia.com

Editor: Upama Biswas
Design: Shashi Bhushan Prasad

ISBN: 978-93-85285-42-4
Publication: 2016

Printed at: Niyogi Offset Pvt. Ltd., New Delhi, India

For my little sis Devina. Hope you start cooking and stop stealing my food now!

Contents

Foreword

Vedant Bahri is an irresistible heady mix of talent and passion put together. This is Vedant in his kitchen.

After a meeting this 'rearing-to-go' teenager's mother, it was almost re-living my childhood. I too began my experiments as early as 7 or 8 years of age and started documenting my recipes ever since. However, mine were anything that was "tasty", while Vedant has churned out food that goes beyond his years.

Being health conscious at such a young age is rare and truly commendable. I have to say that I have discovered some very nice ideas from his book, specially his jar concept.

If this is a creation of a 17-year-old, I wonder what lies ahead! I would like Vedant to reach out to as many youngsters in India and around the globe—to get young minds to think of good food as tasty and healthy and that the two are easily created and not mutually exclusive, to get young minds to use their hands and get to the kitchen rather than buying processed and ready-to-eat junk, to appreciate the flavours of "real" food not steeped with synthetic flavours.

They must look at food, not only as something to fill the stomach or please the taste buds but as a source of nourishment for the mind, body and soul. And at each instance to feel, touch and discover the joy of real food. I realise that Vedant has found the power of food. I noticed he has used Amaranth, "The King of Grains", my compliments to him for he has obviously done his homework discovering forgotten grains.

Well, this book seems to have something for everyone—from snacks, sandwiches and salads to curries and sweet treats. A global collection coming from a Little Master Chef. This is a phenomenal and truly inspirational recipe book. Hobby or profession? There is nothing more powerful than combining passion with talent and making it a profession. Whatever it may be, I can see this foodie is on a fast track, way ahead of his peers and he is surely on the right track as "Health is Wealth". My best wishes Vedant!

Ishi Khosla
2016

Ishi Khosla is a practicing clinical nutritionist, consultant, writer, columnist, researcher, author and an entrepreneur. She has been conferred several awards and recognitions in her field and has also been listed among the 25 Most Powerful Women in the Country by the India Today Group.

Preface

No, I'm not a trained chef or a nutritionist, but a "young eater"—a youngster who loves to cook and, more importantly, EAT. I remember once initially, when I saw an episode of Rachel Allen: Bake! on the television, the apple cake that she baked made my mouth water instantaneously. I knew I had to make it, but the question was how? I had never baked before and didn't know anything about it. That was the first time when I researched on the Internet and baked the same cake in a dhokhla (a popular Indian snack) pan as I didn't possess a cake pan at the time. After that I watched many more episodes, baked even more and started enjoying baking, so much so that my parents decided to turn a little pantry at home into my experimental kitchen. I saved money to buy more gadgets and appliances to add to and better equip my little kitchen with the best baking utensils available.

We often experiment a lot at home with a variety of food served for every meal since my father, mother and sister have their own likes and dislikes. My father likes his food really rich, mom is a little of a health and organic food freak, and my little sister, well, she has no taste buds! It's a chore making her eat. So cooking is kind of a challenge in our house, keeping everyone happy and satiated. However, my experiments go down very well with my family members.

The initial impetus for the book came from the huge response that I got from the blog which I had started writing at 14—The Foodie Journey. My recipes and reviews of restaurants were highly appreciated by my friends and family. An uncle of mine suggested I write a book. At first, the idea seemed absurd; how can a guy whose read 5 books in his life, write his own book? However, after researching and going through many cook books, I felt quite confident and set down to compile the recipes for my book.

But the main concern for me was deciding the kind of recipes that I should offer in the book. What came in handy here was my personal experience with health foods. As a kid and in my early teens, I was a huge fan of junk food. I rarely ate at home and, much to the chagrin of my parents, fast food had become my primary source of sustenance. No wonder, I was chubby throughout school. However, there was a point when I realised the benefit of a healthy lifestyle, thanks to my mother and a few health-conscious teenage friends, I wanted to be "FIT". Since then I've tried almost everything—crash diets, 90-day workout programmes, you name it and I've done it! Unfortunately, nothing worked, until I made an effort to learn about "Health Food". I always thought of health food as boring green vegetables and other things that I hated. But now I realise that health food is actually quite subjective—I consider anything with low amounts of preservatives and processed ingredients as healthy.

Very honestly, I'm the last person you'd expect to eat boring salads and tiny potions all day. Instead I chose to make whatever I want to eat at home. Now, cooking your own food has many advantages—you can control what you put into your body, you can customise ingredients and cheat to make the dish lighter. Initially, I had planned to completely remove all unhealthy ingredients such as sugar, flour, butter, etc. However, I realised that the lack of these ingredients were interfering a bit too much with the taste, so instead of completely removing them, I subtly replaced them with lesser quantities, or healthier ingredients such as unrefined honey, coconut milk or even amaranth flour, and disciplined myself with portion controls. I sat in front of my computer, did a little bit of research, and some amount of mix and match in the kitchen and voila, I had cheat version recipes for all my favourite dishes.

To me, eating healthy wasn't all about getting slim, it was an attempt to not get obese and unhealthy in the future. We see celebrities undergoing massive body transformations in a few weeks. However, the dedication needed to do so is quite inconvenient for regular people like us. Health is not a project, but a way of life. Instead of aiming for quick short-term goals, one should aim for long-term sustainable habits.

As a foodie I can't stand boring, tasteless food. Why should I? Life is too short to not eat what you love. So with a little twisting and substituting the regular ingredients with "healthy" alternatives, I enjoy the best of both worlds. And so should you. With two sections offering more than 70 cheat recipes and another section with interviews of celebs from the film, sports and culinary industries, my aim with this book is to convince youngsters to stop relying on unhealthy fast food and get them into the kitchen, eventually helping them consciously opt for a healthier lifestyle. For youngsters like me who love to cook and experiment, or those keen to learn how to cook, without any of the fuss and keeping health in mind, these recipes are easy, healthy and delicious. So CHEAT IT ALL. Eat all you want and whatever you want, but make it yourself. Cheers and happy reading!

Vedant Bahri

EAT

Health on the Go!

Choosing the healthy way of living is not an easy decision. If you decide to follow it—picking out and preparing the right kind of food can pose a major problem. We all know that we should, simply, eat healthy—lots of green leafy vegetables with regulated amounts of protein and carbohydrates. But healthy food has the reputation of often compromising on taste and variety. Not anymore! As a foodie who also wants to be healthy, I couldn't bear the quintessential "healthy diet food" daily. I missed my sandwiches, burgers and pizzas. So, here I have more than 40 recipes of quick, simple and delicious breakfasts, salads and main dishes that I love to eat— mostly yummy experiments, that my mom and I churn out at home with some inspiration from the Internet (improvised with a personal twist of course). Now say goodbye to boring diet foods and open your eyes to a world of healthy, yet delicious food.

BREAKFAST

The most important meal of the day—BREAKFAST is, unfortunately, the most neglected meal of the day as well (especially by teenagers). There are various reasons for this, the main being the fact that cooking up a healthy breakfast isn't that high on many of our list of priorities after a good, lazy nine-hour sleep. But, be it losing weight or maintaining a healthy lifestyle, the importance of breakfast is far from negligible. From the point of view of nutrition, the gap between the last meal of the day and the first meal the next day, while the human body sleeps through the night, is a very long one indeed, one may say the body fasts during sleep, and it is a known fact that fasting makes one weak and less energetic. Skip breakfast anyone? How do we then survive a whole day ahead without "fuelling our body"? The ideal breakfast, it is suggested by dieticians and health experts, should be had within two hours of waking up to keep the metabolism pepped up, and should also be a source of nourishment for the body—not just fried bacon and eggs everyday (they will ruin you in the long run). The recipes I have provided for breakfast are easy, delicious, quick and some of them can even be made in jars (or bowls) and kept ready a night before.

CHIA MANGO JAR

Makes: 1 jar

A great and tasty breakfast that combines fibre, fruit and sweetened yoghurt. Make it a night before and just grab it from the fridge a minute before digging in after a workout, or just waking up (for my fellow lazy people).

Ingredients

1 tablespoon chia seeds
⅓ cup almond milk
1 tablespoon honey
½ cup vanilla yoghurt or any other flavour
1 mango, cubed
¼ cup raspberries
¼ cup blueberries (keep adding them!)
tender coconut, sliced

Method

1. Soak the chia seeds in the almond milk and honey. I usually soak it for half an hour or one.
2. In a jar or glass layer the soaked and swollen chia seeds first.
3. Then pour the yoghurt and top with mango, berries and coconut!

DID YOU KNOW

Chia seeds are not only a great source of protein and fibre, but are also loaded with many more nutrients—a true superfood.

BERRY PARFAIT

Makes: 1 jar

Just a 4-ingredient breakfast— great start to the day. Like most of the breakfast in jars, this can be made a night before and can be just grabbed from the fridge.

Ingredients

2 tablespoons honey muesli, preferably with nuts
½ cup vanilla yoghurt or any flavour
½ cup chopped fruits of your choice— blueberries, mango, fresh tender coconut, apples, peaches—just go bananas!
1 tablespoon roasted desiccated coconut (optional)

Method

1. In a jar layer the muesli, yoghurt and then the fruits. Add more yoghurt and some more fruits.
2. Top with the desiccated coconut.

DID YOU KNOW

Blueberries are packed with Vitamin C and are rich in antioxidants.

AMARANTH BERRY PUDDING

Makes: 6 single-serving jars or an 8-inch cake pan/dish

Amaranth is a Mexican grain packed with as much protein and fibre as quinoa. This pudding is a great breakfast item for when you have berries in the fridge, and requires no eggs. Also it is pure deliciousness with the ice cream, I guarantee.

Ingredients

Pudding batter

1 cup amaranth flour
¼ cup all-purpose flour
¼ cup oats
2 teaspoons baking powder
1 cup almond milk
1 tablespoon cinnamon powder
2 teaspoons ginger powder
1 teaspoon nutmeg powder
½ cup blueberries
⅔ cup agave or honey
a dash of vanilla

Topping

4 tablespoons raspberries
2 tablespoons water
1 tablespoon honey
1 scoop vanilla ice cream for each serving

Method

1. Preheat the oven at 175°C.
2. Mix all ingredients for the pudding batter in a bowl and keep aside. (you can add the ingredients following the order in which they are listed).
3. Mix and microwave the topping ingredients (except the ice cream) in a bowl for 30 seconds.
4. Pour the batter mixture in a baking dish.
5. Layer the pudding batter with the toppings.
6. Bake for 30 minutes. Scoop out a single portion in a bowl or jar and serve with a scoop of vanilla ice cream.

BREAD PUDDING

Makes: 1 portion

A classic breakfast treat that I love eating at buffets. Bread pudding is basic, tasty and not too fattening either. Enjoy a treat in the morning without worrying about the calories.

Ingredients

3 slices wholewheat bread (sides cut)

Batter

1 egg

1 teaspoon cinnamon powder

¼ cup almond milk, can use normal milk too

1 tablespoon roasted desiccated coconut (optional)

1 teaspoon finely cut dried cranberries or any other dry fruit or nuts (walnuts for me, optional)

1 tablespoon raw honey (can add more if you want it sweeter)

Method

1. Preheat oven at 200°C.
2. Roughly cut the bread slices and spread in a shallow baking dish (I've used a jar here so I can eat my breakfast on the go).
3. Beat the batter ingredients well with a whisk and pour it all over the bread, making sure all the bread is soaked in the batter.
4. Bake in the oven for 15 minutes. Make sure the batter is baked well. Some like it a little moist and some nice and crisp.
5. Serve hot with a chilled custard or maple syrup or like my sister loves it—with vanilla ice cream!

BLUEBERRY AND OATS MUFFINS

Makes: 6 large muffins or 12 cupcakes

Who doesn't love blueberry muffins? They are made with ingredients you probably already have in your pantry and are actually pretty healthy—sounds like a good breakfast to me. These muffins contain a lot of fibre and antioxidants from the oats and berries.

Ingredients

1 cup oats
1 cup flour
½ cup desiccated coconut powder
¾ cup castor sugar
1 cup milk
1 egg
¼ cup coconut oil
1 cup blueberries
1 tablespoon baking powder

Method

1. Preheat oven at 200°C.
2. In a bowl, whisk the all the ingredients together.
3. Pour the batter in a cupcake/muffin tin.
4. Bake for 25 minutes or until golden brown.

CHEF'S TIP

Mix the dry ingredients and the berries in flour first so that it mixes evenly and does not sink to the bottom of the cupcake.

FLAPJACKS

Makes: 1 large 8-inch rectangular cake pan

A sweet British treat, flapjacks are an absolute delight. I personally have very fond memories of them as the first thing I ate during my summer school in the UK was, you guessed it right, flapjacks! They are extremely sweet, chewy and weirdly remind me of brownies.

Ingredients

½ cup melted butter
½ cup brown sugar (dark preferably)
¼ cup golden syrup
3 cups oats
2 tablespoons chopped almonds
1 tablespoon cinnamon powder

Method

1. Preheat oven at 180°C.
2. In a pan, add the melted butter, sugar and golden syrup.
3. Mix and combine the oats, nuts and cinnamon powder.
4. Press into a rectangular cake pan and bake for 20 minutes.
5. Cool for at least 30 minutes.
6. Remove from pan and cut into desired shapes.

DID YOU KNOW

Flapjacks are very rich in calories even though made with mostly healthy ingredients and therefore should be had in small quantities.

MUSHROOM TOAST

Makes: 4

A delight to start your day with, salty herbed mushrooms topped with creamy goats' cheese on a crisp toast—absolutely delicious!

Ingredients

1 teaspoon olive oil
½ teaspoon butter
3 cloves of garlic, crushed
1 cup button mushrooms, sliced
1 teaspoon dried oregano
handful of basil leaves
salt and pepper to taste
1 tablespoon goat cheese
4 slices of any bread of your choice (wholewheat or multigrain preferably)

Method

1. Add the oil and then the butter in a heated saucepan.
2. Once hot, tip in the garlic and cook till lightly fried, then the mushrooms, oregano, chopped basil, salt and pepper.
3. Sauté on high flame for 2–3 minutes.
4. Spread this mix on crisp toasted slices of bread and serve topped with crumbled goat cheese.

GOAT CHEESE AND PRUNES ON TOAST

Makes: 3

My mom's favourite. Gives a nice sweet, nutty taste to the regular goat cheese.

Ingredients

2 prunes
3 walnut halves
2 tablespoons goat cheese
3 slices wholewheat toast, nice and crisp

Method

1. Chop the prunes and walnuts finely.
2. Mix it well with the goat cheese.
3. Spread a thick layer on a crisp toast. And I don't really need to say more! Divine!

DID YOU KNOW:

Prunes are nothing but dried plums—a superfood that aids digestion and also weight loss.

GUACAMOLE ON TOAST

Makes: 3

Guacamole is a Mexican dip. It has avocado which is low in cholesterol and has anti-aging properties. A perfect substitute to mayonnaise and butter! An avocado is ripe when it is darker in colour and feels heavier.

Ingredients

1 ripe avocado (a nice, soft one)
½ onion, chopped
½ tomato, chopped
1 tablespoon chopped coriander
1 tablespoon chopped jalapeno (I like it spicy)
juice of a lemon
salt and pepper to taste
3 slices wholewheat toast, nice and crisp

Method

1. Scoop out the pulp of the avocado and mash it with a fork.
2. Mix the onion, tomato, coriander, jalapeno, lemon juice and the seasoning.
3. Serve on a hot slice of toast or eat as a dip. Experiment!

PEANUT BUTTER FRENCH TOAST

Makes: 4

Cooking this makes the peanut butter gooey and soft from the inside, and the bread becomes crispy. Peanut butter is also pretty healthy–use store-bought or homemade. If you are feeling extra special then use a cocoa hazelnut spread as a topping.

Ingredients

4 slices bread (wholewheat or multigrain, of course it's best made with thick slices of brioche)
2 tablespoons peanut butter (smooth or chunky)
1 tablespoon butter
cocoa hazelnut spread (optional)

Batter

1 egg
¼ cup almond milk
1 teaspoon cinnamon powder
1 tablespoon honey

Method

1. Whisk the batter mixture and keep aside.
2. Spread peanut butter between the slices (sides cut) to make 2 sandwiches. Then cut the sandwiches diagonally to form 4 portions.
3. Coat the sandwich (one at a time) in the batter and put in a hot saucepan with a little butter.
4. On a low flame cook with the butter for around 3–4 minutes, flip the side of the toast and cook the other side the same way till golden and crisp.
5. You can eat it with a light drizzle of honey, maple syrup or the cocoa spread.

CHEF'S TIP

The ideal thickness for the toast should be ¾ to 1 inch thick for it to cook perfectly.

RICOTTA PANCAKES

Makes: 4-5

Seriously, once you go ricotta, you never go back. These pancakes are tender, soft and fluffier than regular pancakes.

Ingredients

Pancake Batter

½ cup flour
½ cup ricotta cheese
2 tablespoons honey
1 egg
⅓ cup almond milk
1 teaspoon lemon zest
1 teaspoon baking powder
cooking spray

Raspberry Compote

1 cup frozen or fresh raspberries (or strawberries)
2 tablespoons honey
1 tablespoon water

Method

1. In a bowl, mix all the ingredients for the compote and microwave for 1-2 minutes.
2. With a hand blender or fork puree this mixture. Cool for half an hour (at least) and set aside.
3. In a large bowl, whisk all ingredients for the pancake batter until smooth.
4. In a hot pan, on medium flame, spray some oil. Drop the batter in circular shapes and cook for 3-4 minutes or until the surface forms bubbles, flip and cook the other side for 2 more minutes or until golden brown.
5. Top the pancakes with the compote and serve.

LEAN ENERGY PANCAKES

Makes: 8

Now this is what I call a guilt-free breakfast. A 3-ingredient pancake that has no sugar, flour, or milk. Yes! I'm not joking. Such a thing does exist, and all credit goes to the amazing fruit—banana. Just banana, oats and egg, it's that simple.

Ingredients

2 large bananas
2 eggs
¼ cup oats
cooking spray

Method

1. Toss all ingredients into a blender and simply blend till a smooth and thick batter is ready.
2. Heat a pan with a thin layer of cooking spray/oil. Add batter and cook for 2–3 minutes or until bubbles form. Flip and cook the other side for another minute or till golden brown.
3. Serve the pancakes with banana slices between layers of the pancake stack and top with loads of honey/ maple syrup—my personal favourite.

DID YOU KNOW

Bananas are an excellent source of instant energy. So ditch your morning caffeine rush and grab a banana instead.

CREPES (SWEET AND SAVOURY)

Makes: 5

Crepes are delicious and usually found on the streets of Paris. As for the fillings, my personal favourite is chocolate, but I also do enjoy the occasional savoury version. This recipe makes a basic unsweetened crepe which can be filled or topped to your liking.

Ingredients

½ cup refined flour
1 tablespoon melted butter
1 egg
¾ cup milk
butter spray

Fillings

Savoury:
sliced ham
sliced cheddar

Sweet:
cocoa hazelnut spread

Method

1. In a bowl, whisk the flour, butter, egg and milk until smooth. Refrigerate this for at least half an hour.
2. Spray a large non-stick pan with a butter spray or melt some butter. Pour a huge spoonful of the batter in the centre of the pan and swirl around to cover the whole pan, on low to medium flame.
3. Cook for 3 minutes or until golden, flip and cook for another 2 minutes.
4. Spread the fillings of your choice and fold.

DID YOU KNOW

In Britain, crepes or pancakes are traditionally eaten with castor sugar and lemon juice as fillings!

BAKED OMELETTE

Makes: 1 big portion

Always land up making scrambled eggs when trying to make an omelette? Well, baking it is the solution. Just pop it in the oven. Flip, slide, dance—whatever you want it to do, it will do, smoothly!

Ingredients

1 teaspoon olive oil
a good sprinkle of cheddar cheese

Egg mix

1 tablespoon chopped red bell pepper
1 tablespoon chopped yellow bell pepper
1 tablespoon chopped mushroom
1 tablespoon chopped onions
1 tablespoon chopped coriander
2 eggs
2 egg whites
salt and pepper to taste

Method

1. Preheat the oven at 200°C.
2. Beat the egg mixture in a bowl and keep aside.
3. Heat oil in a pan, add the beaten egg mixture and cook on medium flame for exactly 1 minute.
4. Remove from flame and sprinkle with cheese.
5. Transfer the pan into the oven and cook for 5 minutes or till the egg fluffs up and the cheese melts. The omelette is ready!

SALADS

A convenient way to enjoy healthy, tasty salads throughout the week, salad in a jar is a trend that is rapidly spreading throughout the world. Sounds too good to be true? I know! Often, due to the unavailability of healthy food, we have no option but to eat out. Perfect for teenagers like myself, or just about everyone who doesn't have the time to prepare nutritious salads daily, but still doesn't want to eat junk, these salads are made in large mason jars (about 16oz or nearly 500ml jar), so they are not only delicious but also filling. Typically, these would last for 2–3 days in the fridge, but with a vacuum sealer for the jars, they can stay fresh for a whole week! The secret to a fresh, long-lasting salad is keeping the dressing as far as possible from the lettuce, starting with the heaviest and the most non-absorbent ingredient at the bottom, working your way up finally to the lighter leaves. So just remember—the dressing goes first, and the lettuce last. I like to leave at least ¼ of my jar empty to stuff in the leaves really tightly. These salad jars are also perfect to take to work or travel with. Even if you don't have jars at hand, just make the salad in a bowl.

BERRY SALAD

Makes: 1 jar

A great, fresh salad that is simple to make and as the name suggests has a fruity side to it. Berries are loaded with antioxidants and walnuts are very healthy.

Ingredients

½ cup strawberries, diced
2 tablespoons blueberries
4 walnuts
1 onion, chopped (optional)
2 tablespoons goat cheese or feta cheese, crumbled
choice of leaves, baby spinach or rocket work well

Berry Vinaigrette Dressing

2 tablespoons olive oil
1 tablespoon balsamic vinegar
1 tablespoon lemon juice
1 tablespoon berry jam (any berry)
1 teaspoon mustard
salt and pepper to taste

Method

1. Whisk all the ingredients for the vinaigrette together in a small bowl.
2. In a mason jar, pour the dressing first.
3. Then, layer with strawberries, blueberries, onion, walnuts.
4. Add the crumbled cheese.
5. Top with the greens, close the jar and refrigerate.

GREEK YOGHURT SALAD

Makes: 1 jar

A very fresh, simple salad. This is one of my favourite, especially in the summers. Not very heavy as I've used hung yoghurt instead of a mayonnaise or a cheese dressing.

Ingredients

8–10 cherry tomatoes
1 small cucumber, diced
2 tablespoons sweet corn kernels
5 black pitless olives
2 tablespoons feta cheese
crisp iceberg lettuce
1 chicken breast (boiled/ poached and shredded, optional)

Greek Dressing

2 tablespoons yoghurt (hung for an hour preferably)
1 tablespoon olive oil
1 clove of garlic, crushed
1 teaspoon honey
salt, pepper and oregano for seasoning

Method

1. Mix all the ingredients for the dressing together in a small bowl.
2. In a jar, put the dressing first.
3. Followed by tomatoes, cucumber, corn, olives, feta cheese, chicken (if using) and lettuce.
4. Make it a night before and enjoy a healthy salad on the go.

KIDNEY BEAN AND CORN SALAD

Makes: 1 jar

A delicious vegetarian Mexican salad recipe. Red beans are an excellent source of protein, and avocados are loaded with nutrients and healthy fats.

Ingredients

1 avocado, diced, toss the diced avocado in the juice of a lemon for that extra flavour
1 onion, diced
½ cup boiled red beans
2 tablespoons sweet corn kernels
8–10 cherry tomatoes
iceberg or romaine lettuce

Mexican Dressing

¼ cup tomato salsa, it can be bought from the market or made fresh at home
3 tablespoons yoghurt (hung for an hour preferably)
salt and pepper to taste

Method

1. Mix the ingredients for the dressing in a bowl.
2. In a mason jar first layer with the dressing.
3. Then add the red beans, tomatoes, diced avocado, corn and top it off with lettuce.
4. Refrigerate on eat directly.

COBB SALAD

Makes: 1 jar

A delicious salad loaded with blue cheese dressing, chicken and bacon. Vegetarians can add kidney beans, chickpeas and corn to make it more wholesome!

Ingredients

8–10 cherry tomatoes
1 avocado, diced
1 chicken breast, boiled or smoked, diced
1 slice bacon, cooked and chopped
romaine or iceberg lettuce

Blue Cheese Dressing

2 tablespoons yoghurt (hung for an hour preferably)
1 teaspoon mayonnaise
1 tablespoon blue cheese, crumbled
Tabasco sauce, few drops
salt and pepper to taste

Method

1. Mix the ingredients for the dressing in a bowl.
2. In a jar or bowl first layer with the dressing.
3. Then add the chicken, bacon, tomatoes, diced avocado and finally lettuce. Ready!

CHICKPEA SALAD

Makes: 1 jar

A very healthy salad with guacamole dressing. Guacamole is also perfect on a nicely toasted slice of bread, with a boiled egg or as a salad dressing!

Ingredients

½ cup boiled chickpeas
8–10 cherry tomatoes
2 tablespoons sweet corn kernels
lettuce

Guacamole dressing

1 ripe avocado
juice of half a lemon
2 tablespoons chopped tomato
2 tablespoons chopped onion
1 tablespoon chopped coriander
salt and pepper to taste

Method

1. Scoop out the flesh from the avocado slicing it into two. Squash it into a rough paste with a fork. Add the rest of the ingredients and mix well to make the guacamole.
2. In a jar, start with the guacamole dressing, followed by boiled chickpeas, tomatoes, corn and lettuce. Dig in!

WATERMELON AND GREEN APPLE SALAD

Makes: 1 portion

A fresh, vibrant salad that is very light in terms of calorie content.

Ingredients

1 cup cubed watermelon
½ green apple, cubed
handful of basil leaves
2 tablespoons balsamic vinegar
1 tablespoon feta cheese
salt and pepper to taste
drizzle of extra virgin olive oil

Method

1. Toss the watermelon and apple together with the basil leaves in a bowl.
2. Sprinkle salt and pepper.
3. Drizzle the olive oil and balsamic vinegar.
4. Crumble the feta cheese.
5. Garnish with the basil leaves and serve.

GRAPEFRUIT AND MANGO SALAD

Makes: 2 portions

A delicious Thai-inspired salad; the flavours—tangy, fresh and exciting.

Ingredients

1 grapefruit or pomelo, peeled
1 ripe mango, cubed
½ cup halved cherry tomatoes
1 spring onion, chopped
¼ cup salted roasted peanuts
¼ cup mint leaves
¼ cup coriander leaves
dollop of feta cheese

Dressing

1 tablespoon tamarind paste
1 tablespoon palm sugar/ brown sugar
1 tablespoon Thai sweet chilli sauce
1 teaspoon lemon juice
salt and pepper to taste

Method

1. Whisk all the dressing ingredients together in a bowl and keep aside.
2. In a salad bowl toss in all the ingredients for the salad except the feta.
3. Drizzle a liberal amount of the dressing and give it a good mix.
4. Crumble the feta on top and serve!

ROAST POTATO SALAD

Makes: 2 portions

Have some pickled veggies lying around, make this smashing salad (even if you don't, this is a great excuse to make some). This salad has a cooling and tangy effect on your palate. Love roasted potatoes, love this even more.

Ingredients

2 cups baby potatoes, cleaned and half-boiled with the peel
1 tablespoon sea salt
1 tablespoon mixed dry herbs
2 tablespoons extra virgin olive oil
1 onion, chopped
handful of mint, chopped
handful of coriander, chopped
4 tablespoons of pickled cucumber and beetroot, finely chopped

Dressing

2 tablespoons hung curd
1 tablespoon feta cheese
1 tablespoon honey
1 clove of garlic, crushed
salt and pepper to taste

Method

1. Whisk all the ingredients for the dressing together and keep aside.
2. Preheat the oven at 180°C.
3. Cut the half-boiled potatoes into halves.
4. Toss them well with salt and mixed dry herbs along with the olive oil in a baking dish.
5. Roast the potatoes in the oven for 20 minutes or till nice and crisp.
6. In a bowl, add the roasted potatoes (I really don't wait for them to cool down, they are so yum), onions, mint and coriander and the pickled cucumber and beetroot.
7. Add the dressing generously, mix and serve!

QUINOA SALAD

Makes: 1 portion

Quinoa is a vegetarian superfood, although not as tasty as white rice, but has amazing amounts of protein, healthy fibre and iron.

Ingredients

½ cup cooked quinoa, (usually takes around 20 minutes to boil depending on the type, just make sure it's washed well)
1 cup baby spinach or rocket leaves (I personally love the little bitter crunch in the rockets)
½ onion, chopped
½ bell pepper, chopped
2 tablespoons boiled corn kernels
2 tablespoons cubed cottage cheese or paneer (feta is good too if you're not watching those calories)

Dressing

1 tablespoon apple cider vinegar
juice of half a lemon
1 tablespoon honey
1 teaspoon wholegrain mustard
1 clove of garlic, crushed
salt and pepper to taste

Method

1. Mix all the dressing ingredients in a bowl and keep aside.
2. Layer a bowl with the quinoa, spinach, followed by chopped onions, bell peppers, corn and paneer.
3. Finally, top it off with the dressing and serve.

CHEF'S TIP:

Make sure that the apple cider vinegar is with the "mother" which is the sediments at the bottom of the bottle. Available in supermarkets.

COUSCOUS SALAD

Makes: 2 portions

Couscous/semolina is a popular alternative to rice and pasta. It is healthy and super quick to make. This is perfect with some grilled chicken or fish and of course a cottage cheese steak for the vegetarians!

Ingredients:

1 cup steamed couscous (just soak some in hot water for half an hour and drain it out once it is fluffy)
½ onion, chopped
½ tomato, chopped or 2–4 cherry tomatoes, halved
½ cup steamed corn kernels
black/green olives
handful of parsley

Dressing

3 tablespoons lemon juice
1 tablespoon honey
1 teaspoon wholegrain mustard
salt and pepper to taste

Method

1. Mix the dressing ingredients in a bowl and keep aside.
2. In a salad bowl, add the couscous, followed by chopped onions and tomatoes, corn, green olives and a handful of chopped fresh parsley. Give it a good toss.
3. Pour in the dressing just before eating and serve.

GRILLED CHICKEN SALAD

Makes: 1 portion

The quickest, easiest salad ever! Especially when you are not in the mood to get all complicated with the marinade or dressing (not that most of my recipes are).

Ingredients

1 boneless chicken breast, flattened
1 teaspoon olive oil
1 clove of garlic, crushed
salt and pepper to taste
handful of salad greens (just any would do)
½ cup cherry tomatoes (whole)
1 tablespoon feta cheese (can add more if you want)

Dressing

1 tablespoon raw apple cider vinegar
juice of a lemon
1 tablespoon raw honey/ or any sweetened fresh fruit jam
1 clove of garlic, crushed
salt and pepper

Method

1. Whisk all the dressing ingredients together and keep aside.
2. In a preheated oven at 185°C, grill the chicken marinated with the oil, garlic and seasoning for 20 minutes or till done.
3. Place the lettuce on a plate, then the cherry tomatoes and the feta
4. Slice the grilled chicken breast and place it on top.
5. Pour the dressing generously and enjoy!

MAINS

The main course, or the most substantial part of a meal is something you cannot compromise with! Ideally, a main course is preceded by a soup and salad and then followed by a dessert. Mains are usually the biggest source of protein in a meal. We "teeneaters", however, have no fixed time of eating and crave all the junk food in the world and mostly blame our lack of time and patience for avoiding healthier options. In India, where I come from, mostly all homes have professional cooks or the mommies do the cooking, so we eat whatever is served. But why not do the cooking for a change? In this section I share few of my favourite main cource recipes. My mains are a whole meal in itself, but I do like to have a salad along with it sometimes. These include a wide variety of vegetarian and non-vegetarian hearty dishes, which make very satisfying lunches or dinners and can be tossed up easily with very few ingredients. I do suggest, though, to plan your meals in advance and make sure all the ingredients are in place before you enter the kitchen.

CHILLI HOT DOG

Makes: 4

My favourite movie theatre snack, hot dogs can be made really well at home. Use an exotic sausage such as chorizo, kielbasa, or Italian to get a smashing hot dog. Although hot dogs can be had with mustard and ketchup only, the chilli gives it the extra burst of taste.

Ingredients

4 hot dog buns
4 sausages of your choice

Chilli

2 tablespoon olive oil
1 onion, chopped
4 cloves of garlic, chopped
2 tablespoons tomato ketchup
2 teaspoons cumin powder
1 tablespoon paprika
salt to taste
1 teaspoon oregano
300 g chicken mince
½ tablespoon chicken stock
1½ cup tomato puree
½ cup water
½ cup boiled kidney beans (optional)

Method

1. To make the chilli, heat some oil in a pan, add the onion and garlic and cook for 3–4 minutes.
2. Then add the ketchup, cumin, paprika, salt, oregano and cook for a minute more.
3. Add the chicken and cook (stirring) for about 5–6 minutes or until cooked.
4. Pour in the stock, puree, water and beans, cook for 5–10 more minutes on high flame or until the sauce thickens.
5. To steam the buns, slit the buns sideways (about ¾ of the way in). Put a glass of water and a plate containing the buns inside the microwave and heat for 30 seconds.
6. Assemble the sausage inside the slit made earlier in the bun and top with the chilli to serve.

MEATBALL MARINARA SUB

Makes: 4

I don't think I can express my love for this sandwich in words—I absolutely love it. I use a lean and healthy meat (mostly chicken) for my meatballs, and no additional ingredients at all. My super quick marinara sauce perfectly flavours the meatballs.

Ingredients

2 tablespoons white oil
500 g chicken mince
1 egg
½ cup breadcrumbs
salt and pepper to taste
4 hot dog buns
mozzarella cheese (fresh or processed), also as little as possible

Marinara sauce

4 cloves of garlic, chopped
1 onion, finely chopped
salt to taste
400 g tomato puree
½ cup water
1 tablespoon sugar
1 teaspoon chilli powder
handful of basil leaves, finely shredded
American mustard

Method

1. In a pan, heat the oil while you mix together the chicken mince, egg, breadcrumbs, salt and pepper in a bowl.
2. Shape this mix into small balls and drop into the pan. Then cook while gently moving balls for 4 minutes (they should only be semi-cooked). Remove and keep aside.
3. In the same pan, cook the garlic, onion and salt in the oil for about 3–4 minutes. Add the ingredients for the marinara sauce and stir.
4. Cook sauce for another 3–4 minutes till it thickens. Add the meatballs into the sauce and cook for 5–6 minutes until cooked.
5. Slice the hot dog buns, and put some meatballs and top with mozzarella cheese. Bake for 5–6 minutes at 200°C until the cheese has melted.

CHICKEN SALAD SANDWICH

Makes: 1

The classic chicken salad sandwich! Never get bored again—zingy, tangy, garlicky, creamy—perfection! Also, did I mention lower calories?

Ingredients

- 1 ciabatta bread (slit sideways in the middle)
- 1 large chicken breast, roasted or boiled and shredded with a fork or fingers
- ⅓ cup hung curd/yoghurt
- 2 tablespoons soft cheese (goat cheese, feta or whatever is available)
- 2 cloves of garlic, crushed
- 1 tablespoon lemon juice
- 1 teaspoon raisins
- sun-dried tomato pesto (store-bought or made by grinding sun-dried tomato with some oil)
- handful of rocket leaves

Method

1. Toast the bread in the oven.
2. In a bowl, mix the chicken, yoghurt, cheese, garlic, lemon juice and raisins.
3. Smear some pesto on the top half of the bread. Place the chicken and the rocket leaves on the lower half and then press together with the top half.

CHEF'S TIP:

The reason behind shredding the chicken or flaking the chicken with a fork is to not let the juices ooze out so that the flavours stay intact.

CAPRESE TOASTIE

Makes: 1

When people think of Italy, they think of pizza. But although this sandwich is my own creation, it represents Italy for me. Like the pizza margherita, this sandwich contains the colours of the Italian flag—red, white and green. This sandwich is definitely a more filling and upgraded version of the Italian Insalata Caprese.

Ingredients

1 tablespoon olive oil
2 large tomatoes, halved and then cut vertically
handful of fresh basil leaves
1 small ciabatta roll or half of a large one.
fresh buffalo mozzarella (preferably Bocconcini)

Method

1. Preheat oven at 200°C.
2. Heat oil in a small pan and add the tomatoes. Keep stirring as tomatoes can stick very easily.
3. After tomatoes have softened, about 5 minutes in, turn off the heat and add torn basil leaves and give it a mix.
4. Cover the pan with cling film and let it cool for a while to let the flavours gain strength.
5. Slice bread from the middle and layer with tomatoes and then thin slices of cheese. Bake in the oven at the highest temperature just till the cheese melts and the bread becomes golden brown.

CHICKEN PITA POCKET

Makes: 4

A no-fuss recipe, this will be loved by kids and adults alike. The basic vegetables used to accompany the chicken add amazing freshness to the dish and it is served in a soft pita with a garlic yoghurt dip. Although the chicken can be cooked immediately, marinating it overnight leads to softer, more succulent pieces of chicken.

Ingredients

2 chicken breasts
2 tablespoons fresh parsley
1 teaspoon ground cumin
1 teaspoon ground coriander
1 tablespoon lemon juice
salt to taste
1 tablespoon minced garlic
2 tablespoons hung curd or yoghurt
1 tablespoon oil
2 pita bread (wholewheat)
1 tomato, sliced
½ cucumber, sliced
1 onion, sliced

Dip

½ cup hung curd/yoghurt
5 cloves of garlic, minced
juice of a lemon
salt and pepper to taste

Method

1. Cut chicken into bits or strips. Toss in a bowl with parsley, spices, lemon juice, salt, garlic and curd and keep aside for at least 15 minutes or you may keep it ready the day before and leave it in the fridge overnight for better results.
2. Mix all the dip ingredients in a bowl and leave it in the fridge to chill.
3. In a pan, heat some oil and sauté the chicken for 6 minutes or until cooked.
4. Cut the pita bread into half. Put chicken, tomato, cucumber and onion into the pita pocket and top with the chilled dip.

CHICKEN AND MANGO SALSA WRAP

Makes: 1

The secret to any good wrap is using the freshest ingredients possible. Fresh mozzarella is not only healthier than processed cheese but is also tastier. But the fresh basil is what makes this wrap explode with flavour.

Ingredients

1 wholewheat/corn tortilla
1 smoked chicken breast, cut in thin strips
2 tablespoons mango salsa
feta cheese crumble (the more, the yummier)

Method

1. Heat the tortilla in the microwave for 15 seconds.
2. Mix the chicken and mango salsa.
3. Spread it on the tortilla.
4. Crumble some feta.
5. Role it and devour!

PAD THAI

Makes: 4 portions

A quick to toss up dish, Pad Thai is perhaps one of the most iconic Thai dishes. It is absolutely delicious and is packed with a lot of health benefits as well. Instead of making a sauce from scratch, it is more convenient to just add store-bought sauce.

Ingredients

2 chicken breasts
1 tablespoon white oil
3 cloves of garlic, chopped
4 eggs
375 g flat rice noodles (soaked in hot water for 15 minutes)
½ cup Pad Thai sauce (tamarind paste, palm sugar, lemon grass, soy sauce and fish sauce)
½ cup bean sprouts
½ tablespoon salt
½ cup spring onion, chopped
juice of a lemon
1 tablespoon chilli powder
2 tablespoons crushed peanuts

Method

1. Beat the chicken breasts with a rolling pin or a pan to flatten them. Slice into thin slices.
2. In a wok or pan, heat some oil and add the garlic. When the oil is hot enough, add the chicken and keep stirring it around until the chicken turns white-golden in colour, for about 3–5 minutes.
3. Remove the chicken and keep aside on a plate. Crack 4 eggs into the pan and keep mixing until the eggs are scrambled. Add the noodles and then the sauce.
4. To this, quickly stir in the sprouts, salt, spring onion, chicken, lemon juice, chilli powder and peanuts. Mixing to incorporate all the elements, cook for about 3–4 minutes and serve.

Garlic Pasta

Makes: 2 portions

One of the quickest recipes I have ever tried, this pasta is perfect for weekdays when you have no idea what to cook. Inspired by the Spaghetti aglio e olio, the addition of cherry tomatoes takes this dish to a new level and also makes for a nutritious meal.

Ingredients

1 tablespoon olive oil
4–5 cloves of garlic, crushed
1 teaspoon chilli flakes
2 cups cherry tomatoes, halved
salt and pepper to taste
handful of basil leaves
3 cups penne pasta, boiled and drained

Method

1. Heat oil in a saucepan, add garlic and chilli flakes and stir for about a minute.
2. Add the salt and cherry tomatoes, keep stirring for about 2–3 minutes.
3. Add the roughly torn basil leaves.
4. Then simply add the pasta and keep stirring until the sauce coats the pasta.
5. Remove from flame and add loads of fresh crushed pepper.

(I love to toss in some ham or smoked chicken cubes to satisfy my hardcore non-vegetarian taste buds)

SPAGHETTI BOLOGNESE

Makes: 2 portions

Traditionally, Spaghetti Bolognese is started off by sautéing a soffritto (onion, carrot, celery) and is gently simmered for hours. Furthermore, it is cooked with red meat such as beef or veil. My version is much more convenient to make—takes about half an hour to cook, fewer ingredients and is also healthier as I use chicken (a leaner meat).

Ingredients

1 tablespoon olive oil
1 onion, finely chopped
3 cloves of garlic, finely chopped
salt and pepper to taste
1 teaspoon cumin seeds
1 teaspoon chilli powder
250 g chicken mince (soya granules for vegetarians, soaked and drained)
1½ cup fresh tomato puree
½ cup water
1 tablespoon honey
1 tablespoon thyme
handfull of basil, roughly torn
250 g spaghetti, cooked
parmesan cheese for garnishing

Method

1. Heat some oil in a saucepan and sauté onion and garlic. Add salt, pepper, cumin and chilli powder and cook for about 2–3 minutes or until onions soften.
2. Add the mince (chicken or soya) and keep stirring while cooking for about 5–7 minutes.
3. Add the tomato puree, water, honey and thyme and let it simmer for about 15–20 minutes or until sauce thickens. Stir in a few basil leaves.
4. In a pasta plate, place the boiled spaghetti and pour the minced chicken/soya sauce over it.
5. Garnish with basil leaves and grated parmesan cheese.

GOAN PRAWN CURRY

Makes: 3 portions

Spicy, tangy, sweet and delicious, this is one of my favourite curries. This curry isn't very authentic—tried to add a twist of my own. Although this dish is quite simple to make. The curry paste can be made using fresh spices or dry powder.

Ingredients

2 tablespoons white oil
2 onions, chopped
2 tomatoes, chopped
½ cup water
500 g small prawns
salt to taste

Curry Paste

1 teaspoon cumin seeds
1 teaspoon mustard seeds
5 cloves of garlic
1-inch ginger cube
1 teaspoon whole black peppercorns
few 1-inch cinnamon sticks
5 cloves
6 dried Kashmiri red chilies
½ teaspoon turmeric
handful of curry leaves
½ cup white vinegar

Method

1. In a mixer add all the spices and vinegar for the curry and grind to form a smooth paste.
2. In a frying pan or wok, heat some oil and add the onions, tomatoes and some salt, cook till the onions lose colour and are beginning to brown and have softened.
3. Add the paste and cook while stirring for about another 3–4 minutes on a high flame, to get rid of the rawness.
4. Add the prawns and the water. Put a lid on and let it cook for 10–15 minutes on a low flame till the prawns are cooked and the gravy has reduced. Remember not to over cook the prawns.
5. Serve with brown rice or quinoa.

HONEY CHICKEN

Makes: 4 portions

Honey chicken is perhaps one of the most popular Chinese takeout dish in the world; it also happens to be my favourite. Now I have realised that honey chicken isn't very healthy—it's fried and has a lot of sugar content. My recipe requires no frying and very less sugar.

Ingredients

3 skinless chicken breasts, cut into 1-inch cubes
1 egg
½ cup flour
1 teaspoon salt
2 tablespoons oil
2 spring onions, chopped
1 onions cubed
1 green bell pepper, cubed
1 tablespoon sesame seeds

Honey Garlic Sauce

½ cup water + 1 tablespoon cornstarch (mixed)
½ cup apple juice
5 cloves of garlic, crushed
2 tablespoons soy sauce
¼ cup vinegar
3 tablespoons ketchup
½ cup honey
1 teaspoon chili powder
1 teaspoon salt

Method

1. In a bowl, mix the chicken cubes with the egg. In a ziplock bag, mix this chicken, flour, salt and shake until all cubes are coated.
2. Heat oil in a wok and stir fry the chicken for 4–5 minutes or until the chicken is golden brown.
3. In another frying pan, mix all the ingredients for the sauce and cook for 5 minutes or until the sauce thickens.
4. Add the chicken and veggies with the sesame seeds into the sauce and mix well. Cook for 4–5 minutes and remove from flame. Serve hot with boiled rice, ideally, but for a healthier option you may go for quinoa.

PESTO QUINOA

Makes 3 portions

A quick, easy to toss up dinner or lunch. Quinoa is packed with protein, but is quite bland on its own, however, this dish makes it fun.

Ingredients

1 tablespoon olive oil
3 cloves of garlic, crushed
2 tablespoons basil pesto
1 cup halved cherry tomatoes
3 cups boiled quinoa (1 cup raw quinoa makes 3 cups boiled quinoa)
¼ cup grated smoked mozzarella
2 smoked chicken breasts cut in cubes (optional) or choice of vegetables
salt and pepper to taste
parmesan cheese for garnishing

Method

1. Heat some oil in a wok. Stir fry the garlic, basil pesto and cherry tomatoes for 2 minutes in the oil.
2. Add the boiled quinoa and then the mozzarella and give it a quick toss so the cheese melts and mixes well.
3. Add the salt and pepper and the chicken/veggies.
4. Garnish with parmesan cheese and serve!

GRILLED PRAWNS WITH PANKO

Serves: 4 (or 2 if it's me eating!)

These prawns are extremely delicious, crispy and tender at the same time. Panko is nothing but Japanese breadcrumbs. Vegetarians can try the same with tofu or mozzarella sticks! Best served with tamarind sauce or Thai sweet chilli sauce.

Ingredients

8 large prawns, deshelled and deveined
1 cup flour
2 eggs, beaten
1 cup panko
1 teaspoon garlic powder
salt and pepper to taste
1 lemon wedge

Method

1. Preheat oven at 200°C.
2. Pat dry the deveined prawns.
3. Mix the panko with the salt and garlic powder and keep aside.
4. Dust the prawns with the flour, dip it nicely in the egg and coat it thickly with the panko crumbs. Do this individually for all the prawns.
5. Coat the baking tray with a light spray of olive oil, place the prawns on the tray.
6. Transfer the tray to the preheated oven and grill the prawns for 10-15 minutes. The crispiest, yummiest prawns are ready! Squeeze some lemon juice and serve. I love eating these with the Thai grapefruit and mango salad.

HONEY MUSTARD CHICKEN

Makes: 2 portions

A great recipe to tang up a boring chicken breast. Sweet, sour and a well-cooked piece of lean chicken—healthy, tasty and simple to make. I've personally observed that baked chicken is juicier than pan-cooked chicken, so I prefer to bake it, although it takes a bit more time, it ensures a well-cooked chicken breast.

Ingredients

3 tablespoons honey
2 teaspoons mustard
1 teaspoon oregano
1 teaspoon dried parsley
1 teaspoon paprika
1 tablespoon oil
2 skinless chicken breasts
salt and pepper to taste

Method

1. Preheat oven to 175°C.
2. In a small bowl, mix the herbs, honey, mustard and oil to make the honey mixture.
3. Season the chicken breast with salt and pepper and rub in half of the honey mixture.
4. Bake for 30 minutes and brush or drizzle with the remaining mixture and then bake for another 10-15 minutes on the other side.
5. Serve with boiled veggies to make it even healthier and more filling.

LEAN BARBEQUE CHICKEN

Makes: 3 portions

This chicken is moist, spicy and tangy—extremely tasty and very simple to make. A huge fan of barbeque pork and beef dishes, the chicken version never really appealed to me until I actually tried it. It's very tasty and is much less fattening and healthier than red meat.

Ingredients

½ cup any sweet barbeque sauce
3 chicken breasts (skinless, bone in)

Spice mix

2 teaspoons fennel seeds
1 teaspoon cumin powder
2 teaspoon smoked paprika
½ tablespoon brown sugar
salt to taste

Method

1. Preheat oven at 180°C.
2. Mix all spices together and rub on the chicken breasts and keep aside for an hour or so (refrigerate overnight to infuse flavours).
3. Place the chicken breasts on a foiled baking tray.
4. Bake for 30 minutes. Take out of the oven and baste with the barbeque sauce (with a brush or spoon).
5. Bake again for 5 minutes and serve.

MUSHROOM CHICKEN

Makes: 3 portions

Healthy and filling, this recipe combines chicken breasts with herbed mushrooms–a delicious combination. Makes a great dinner or lunch and can be served with steamed veggies or some quinoa.

Ingredients

½ cup flour
salt and pepper to taste
3 chicken breasts (pounded until thin)
4 tablespoons olive oil
250 g button mushrooms, quartered
few sprigs of thyme (dried or fresh)
⅓ cup chicken broth (or vegetable) can make it with the cubes easily available.
few sprigs of fresh parsley/coriander

Method

1. Season the flour with salt and pepper. Coat a thin layer onto both sides of the chicken (shaking off excess).
2. In a pan, heat 2 tablespoons of oil. Brown the chicken breasts for about 4–5 minutes on each side.
3. Remove chicken from pan and keep aside.
4. In the same pan, heat 2 tablespoons of oil and add the mushrooms. Stir fry with thyme, salt and pepper, for 5 minutes.
5. Add the broth, cook for 5 minutes on low heat. Put the chicken breasts in the pan and let the flavours mix on a medium flame for about 3 minutes.
6. Garnish with parsley and serve.

GLAZED LAMB CHOPS

Makes: 4 portions

Sweet, sticky and meaty—these lamb chops are simple and delicious. My alternative to smoked pork ribs; this is not for those people who are in a rush. Slow cooking makes all the difference in the world! Try this only if you have patience and more than that...super taste buds!

Ingredients

500 g lamb chops
1 litre apple juice
3 star anise
1½ teaspoon salt
2 tablespoon honey
1 tablespoon chilli powder

Method

1. Put the lamb chops, apple juice, star anise and salt in a deep-bottomed saucepan or wok and after bringing it to a boil on high flame, let it simmer on a low heat for 40 minutes (with a lid).
2. Increase the flame and cook for 10 more minutes or until the sauce is dry.
3. Transfer the lamb in a baking dish.
4. Mix the honey and red chilli well and brush the mixture on the chops.
5. Bake for 10 minutes at 200°C. Dig into the stickiest, yummiest lamb chops ever.

KEEP
CALM
AND
COOK
ON

TREAT

It's ok to sin once in a while!

Here comes the favourite part—BURGERS, PIZZAS and DESSERTS! Also the main reason why I am writing this book. All the fast food easily available with the promise of a 30-minute delivery time really makes us lazy and impatient to cook a healthy meal, especially after a packed day studying, outdoors or at work, who really wants to start cooking when you have the option of eating all the junk you stock up in your kitchen or order out! Well, the good news is that there ARE alternatives—yummier, healthier and super-fast to churn up. Like I mentioned before, I'm not a trained chef, just a passionate foodie. So I share here my favourite combos—super healthy and super easy. All you have to do is stock up the kitchen with all ingredients on a weekend (I have provided a shopping list at the end of the book). And trust me, once you get the hang of it, you just need an excuse to make your favourite food at home.

BURGERS, PIZZAS, SLIDERS AND SIDES

I always try to use fresh ingredients for the burgers and pizzas. Another way to cut down on the carb content is by using slider buns or even small pita breads for the burgers with the patties grilled instead of frying them. Although it is quite simple to make a wholewheat pizza bread, the most convenient and fastest way (also ensure that you eat more veggies and meats as compared to the bread) is using wholewheat tortilla as the base. These are light and crisp and super quick! A person like me with a big appetite, definitely needs the sides along—so no fries but lots of healthier options. Here you go!

MOROCCAN LAMB BURGER

Makes: 4

An exotic lamb burger with Middle Eastern flavours. The Harissa paste is a MUST for this as it provides a unique flavour.

Ingredients

4 burger buns
1 tomato, sliced
4 slices of gherkins
crisp lettuce

Patty

600 g lamb mince
1 red onion, chopped finely
2 cloves of garlic, crushed
1 teaspoon cumin powder
1 tablespoon paprika
2 eggs
salt and pepper to taste
2 tablespoon olive oil

Dip

½ cup hung curd
2 cloves crushed garlic
2 tablespoons finely chopped mint
1 teaspoon harissa paste (can be found in a supermarket)
¼ cup cucumber, grated

Method

1. Take the lamb mince in a bowl and break the eggs into it. Add the onion, garlic, cumin, paprika, salt and pepper and mix well. Keep aside.
2. Take ¼ of the mince and flatten into a thick patty. Repeat for the rest.
3. Heat oil in a frying pan and fry the patty for 7 minutes on one side without flipping to make sure that juices are sealed in. Cook on the other side for 5–7 minutes (on medium heat) or until brown.
4. While frying the patty, take the hung curd in a bowl and mix well with the garlic, mint, harissa paste and grated cucumber and keep aside.
5. Slice the buns and toast until golden brown.
6. Place the patty on the bun base and top with the lettuce, tomato slices and gherkin.
7. Spread the dip on the bun top and gently press together.

BLUE CHEESE BURGER

Makes: 4 portions

A delicious, juicy chicken patty stuffed with sharp blue cheese.

Ingredients

4 sesame burger buns
iceberg lettuce (optional)
1 large tomato, sliced (optional)
4 slices of gherkins (optional)
4 tablespoons mayonnaise (low-fat)

Patty

600 g chicken mince (lean)
1 tablespoon garlic paste
2 eggs
handful of coriander or parsley
salt and pepper to taste
4 tablespoons blue cheese
2 tablespoons olive oil

Method

1. In a bowl, mix the chicken mince with garlic paste, eggs, parsley and salt and pepper to taste. Keep aside covered with cling wrap.
2. Preheat oven at 200°C.
3. Take ¼ of the mince and flatten into a thin circle.
4. Place ¼ of the cheese into the centre of the patty. Fold the edges and form into a thick patty ball.
5. Flatten just a little, making sure the cheese is enclosed. Repeat for the 3 other patties.
6. Place the patties on a baking tray, brush some olive oil and grill for 20 minutes. Flip and grill for another 10 minutes.
7. Slice the buns (sidewise) into two and toast it lightly in a frying pan.
8. Place the patty on the bun base and top with the lettuce, tomatoes and pickle.
9. Spread the mayo on the bun top and complete assembling the burgers.

CRISPY CHICKEN BURGER WITH LEMON MAYONNAISE

Makes: 4

A great quick chicken burger with a zingy, tangy sauce.

Ingredients

- 4 wholewheat burger buns
- 1 tomato, sliced
- 1 gherkin, sliced
- 4 slices of cheddar cheese (optional)
- 4 strips of bacon (optional)

Crispy Chicken Patty

- 4 thinly pounded chicken breasts
- 2 cups breadcrumbs
- 1 teaspoon paprika
- 1 teaspoon salt
- 2 cups flour
- 2 eggs, beaten
- 2 tablespoons olive oil

Lemon Mayonnaise

- 2 tablespoons low-fat mayonnaise
- 1 teaspoon lemon juice with a little of the lemon zest
- ½ teaspoon onion powder

Method

1. In a bowl, season and mix the breadcrumbs with the paprika and salt.
2. Dip the chicken breasts one by one, in the flour (dust off excess), then dip in the whisked egg and then coat them with the breadcrumbs.
3. In a pan, heat the oil and cook the patties for 4–5 minutes on each side until golden brown and cooked. You can also grill these instead, lightly brushed with olive oil in a preheated oven at 180°C for around 15 minutes each side or till golden and crisp.
4. For the lemon mayo, add the lemon juice to the low-fat mayo along with the onion powder and mix well. Grate in some lemon zest.
5. Toast the buns in the oven grill.
6. On the bun base, place the tomato slice, gherkin, patty, followed by the mayo. Finally, gently press with the bun top.

FISH FILLET BURGER

Makes: 4

Hands down, the best burger ever! This, coming from a guy who isn't so fond of eating fish.

Ingredients

4 burger buns
4 tablespoons tartar sauce or mayonnaise mixed with chopped pickles and lemon juice
4 slices cheddar cheese (optional)

Fish patty

2 cups breadcrumbs
1 teaspoon thyme
1 teaspoon garlic powder
1 teaspoon salt
4 fillets of any white fish
2 cups flour
2 eggs, whisked
cooking spray

Method

1. Preheat oven at 200°C.
2. Mix the breadcrumbs, thyme, salt and garlic powder in a bowl.
3. To start, coat the fillets into the flour (please make sure the fillets are dried first on a kitchen towel), then dip it in the egg, and coat again with the seasoned breadcrumbs (dusting off the excess).
4. Place the fillets on an oiled baking sheet and bake for 10 minutes. Flip and bake for another 5–7 minutes.
5. Slice the burger bun and toast it.
6. Place the fillet on the bun base and top with a tablespoon of the tartar/ mayo and cheese and gently press with the bun top.

BBQ CHICKEN AND CARAMELISED ONION BURGER

Makes: 4

The star of this burger is the caramelised onion, which makes it sort of sweet. Perfect with the smokey BBQ chicken.

Ingredients

4 burger buns
4 slices cheese
1 tomato, sliced
handful of iceberg lettuce

Patty

600 g chicken mince
2 tablespoons smokey BBQ sauce (store-bought is perfect)
2 dashes Tabasco sauce (more if you like it hot!)
salt to taste
2 tablespoons olive oil

Caramelised Onions

2 large onions, sliced
2 tablespoons BBQ sauce
1 tablespoon brown sugar

Method

1. In a bowl, mix the chicken with the BBQ sauce, Tabasco sauce and salt.
2. Form these into 4 equal patties.
3. In a small pan heat some oil, sauté the onions and BBQ sauce and sugar for 5–6 minutes or until they are caramelised and keep aside.
4. In a larger pan, heat the oil. Cook chicken patties over medium heat for 6 minutes on each side or until golden brown.
5. Top the bun base with the lettuce, tomato, burger patty, cheese and then the caramelised onions and gently press with the bun top.

FALAFEL AND HUMMUS PITA SLIDER

Makes: 4

Loaded with chickpeas, these burgers are hearty, healthy and delicious. The dressing is fresh, tangy and refreshing.

Ingredients

8 mini pita bread
2 tablespoons hummus
2 tablespoons Greek yoghurt dressing
4 slices pickled cucumber and beetroot

Falafel

1½ cups boiled black chickpea
1 onion, finely chopped
handful of chopped coriander (with the stem as the stem has the most flavour)
1 teaspoon garlic paste
1 teaspoon ginger paste
2 slices of bread, soaked in water and squeezed
1 teaspoon cumin, roasted and ground
1 teaspoon chat masala
salt and pepper to taste
½ cup sesame seeds
3 tablespoons olive oil

Method

1. In a mixer, add the chickpeas, onion, coriander, garlic, ginger, bread, salt, pepper, cumin and chat masala with 2 tablespoons of olive oil to form a smooth paste.
2. Make round patties according to the size of your sliders. In a plate, pour out the sesame seeds. Then dab both sides of the patty on the plate to coat the patty evenly.
3. Place the patties on the oven tray, brush lightly on both sides with olive oil and bake for 10 minutes in a preheated oven at 200°C, flip sides and bake for another 10 minutes or till done.
4. On a lightly toasted mini pita bread, spread yoghurt dip then the patty, pickled cucumber and beetroot with a spoonful of the hummus. Press together with another mini pita.

BBQ RUB TOFU PITA SLIDER

Makes: 4

Tofu, made with soybeans, is one of the best vegetarian source of protein with very little calories and has no cholesterol. These barbeque sliders have a combination of amazing flavours—a spiced rub and a sweet BBQ sauce.

Ingredients

8 mini pita bread
2 tablespoons blue cheese yoghurt dip
handful of rocket leaves
200 g tofu sliced into four 1-inch slices
4 tablespoons barbeque sauce

BBQ rub

½ tablespoon wholegrain mustard
½ teaspoon onion powder
½ teaspoon garlic powder
1 teaspoon paprika
1 teaspoon cumin powder

Method

1. Preheat oven at 175°C.
2. In a bowl, mix all the rub ingredients and keep aside.
3. Coat the tofu in the rub and place it on a baking tray and put it in the oven for 25 minutes, flipping after 15 minutes.
4. Spoon the BBQ sauce on both sides of the tofu and grill for another 5 minutes.
5. Place the tofu on the lightly toasted mini pita bread followed by rocket leaves and the blue cheese dip. Press together with another mini pita.

BROCCOLI AND QUINOA PITA SLIDER

Makes: 4

Broccoli and quinoa—both superfoods! For those who find this too healthy, trust me, this is divine and sinful!

Ingredients

8 mini pita bread

Broccoli and quinoa patty

1 medium broccoli flower, blanched
¾ cup boiled quinoa
4 cloves of garlic
1 onion, chopped
2 tablespoons grated cheddar cheese
2 tablespoons grated parmesan cheese
salt and pepper to taste
1 cup flour
1 egg
2 cups breadcrumbs/ panko

Guacamole

1 ripe avocado
Juice of half lemon
½ a tomato, chopped
½ an onion, chopped
chopped coriander
salt to taste

Method

1. Mash the broccoli, quinoa, garlic, onion, cheeses and the seasoning well in a mixer to make a smooth thick paste.
2. Make 4 equal patties with the mix, dip in flour, then whipped egg and coat with the breadcrumbs (dust off the excess).
3. Place them in a preheated oven at 200°C after brushing lightly with olive oil. Bake for 10 minutes, flip and bake for another 10 minutes. The yummiest cheesy super healthy broccoli patties!
4. In the meanwhile, scoop out the flesh from the avocado slicing it into two. Squash it into a rough paste with a fork. Add the lemon juice, chopped tomatoes, onions, coriander and salt. Mix well.
5. Place the patty on the lightly toasted mini pita bread and top with guacamole. Press together with another mini pita.

RED KIDNEY BEAN AND OATS PITA SLIDER

Makes: 4

A protein-rich veggie burger with a lots of fibre too. Easy to make and delicious!

Ingredients

8 mini pita bread
handful of lettuce

Patty

1½ cup boiled red kidney beans
½ cup oats
1 onion, finely chopped
3 cloves of garlic, crushed
1 teaspoon paprika
1 teaspoon roasted cumin
salt and pepper to taste
handful of parsley
2 tablespoons olive oil

Sauce 1

1 tablespoon ketchup
1 tablespoon wholegrain mustard

Sauce 2 (optional)

1 tablespoon hung yoghurt
1 tablespoon feta cheese
1 teaspoon honey
1 clove of garlic, crushed
½ an onion, finely chopped
chopped coriander
salt and pepper to taste

Method

1. Preheat oven at 200°C.
2. Mix the beans, oats, onion, garlic, paprika, cumin, salt, pepper and parsley in a mixer with 2 tablespoons of olive oil to form a paste (doesn't have to be too smooth).
3. Make cakes according to the size of your burger buns/pita bread.
4. Place them on the oven tray, brush lightly on both sides with olive oil.
5. Bake for 15 minutes, flip sides and bake for another 10 minutes or till done.
6. In the meanwhile, in two separate bowls, whisk together the 2 different sauce ingredients and keep aside.
7. On lightly toasted small pita bread, spread sauce 1, some crunchy lettuce, then the patty and sauce 2 (optional). Press together with another mini pita.

SWEET POTATO PITA SLIDER WITH BLUE CHEESE SAUCE

Makes: 6

The little sweetness from the sweet potato and the strong blue cheese "tang" in the dressing gives it a very distinct flavour and taste. You can also serve it as small balls for a party snack!

Ingredients

12 mini pita breads or 6 slider buns

Patty

1 large sweet potato, boiled or baked
½ cup boiled red beans
½ cup boiled rice
1 tablespoon of chopped walnuts
½ an onion, chopped
1 teaspoon cumin powder
1 teaspoon paprika
1 green chilli
salt and pepper to taste
2 tablespoons oil

Sauce

½ cup hung yoghurt
1 tablespoon honey
1 tablespoon blue cheese
salt and pepper to taste

Method

1. Preheat oven at 200°C.
2. Mix the sweet potato, beans, rice, walnuts, onion, cumin, paprika, green chilli, salt and pepper in a mixer to form a coarse paste.
3. Make cakes according to the size of your burger buns/pita bread. Place them on the oven tray, brush lightly on both sides with olive oil.
4. Bake for 15 minutes, flip sides and bake for another 10–15 minutes or till done.
5. In the meanwhile, in a bowl, whisk together yoghurt, honey, blue cheese, salt and pepper to form a smooth sauce.
6. On a lightly toasted small pita bread or slider bun, spread the sauce, then the patty. You could add caramelised onions for that extra crunch or the pickled cucumber and beetroot.

TOMATO AND BASIL PIZZA

Makes: 1

A recipe so easy, even a 2-year-old could do it! A no-fuss pizza with just a few ingredients.

Ingredients

1 large wholewheat tortilla
1 large tomato or 8–10 cherry tomatoes, thinly sliced
1 tablespoon olive oil
8–10 pitted olives
4 cloves of garlic, crushed
2 tablespoon feta cheese
handful of basil

Method

1. Preheat oven at 220°C.
2. In a bowl, mix together the tomatoes, olives and garlic. Drizzle some olive oil. Let this marinate for at least 30 minutes in the fridge.
3. Pour on top of the tortilla and bake for 12–14 minutes.
4. To serve, crumble and sprinkle the feta and throw in a few basil leaves.

PESTO AND FETA VEG PIZZA

Makes: 1

My secret to a low-calorie pizza and also a cheat is using tortilla instead of regular dough—this makes a pizza crisp and takes lesser time to bake; plus a thin crust every time! Also as mozzarella is usually quite high in fat, I try to avoid it unless necessary. This is something quite different from the traditional tomato sauce-based pizza, it's a great combination of salty, sweet and creamy flavours.

Ingredients

- 1 large wholewheat tortilla
- 2 tablespoons pesto sauce
- 1 large onion, sliced (sautéed with a tablespoon of oil and a teaspoon of sugar for 5 minutes)
- ½ cup sliced red and yellow bell peppers
- 8–10 pitted black olives
- 1 tablespoon sweet corn kernels
- 2 tablespoons feta cheese

Method

1. Preheat oven at 220°C.
2. Place the tortilla on a baking tray, spread the sauce, and sprinkle the toppings except the feta cheese.
3. Bake for 12–14 minutes or until the crust is golden.
4. Take the pizza out of the oven, crumble and sprinkle the feta and serve!

BBQ BLUE CHEESE CHICKEN PIZZA

Makes 1

The sweetness from the barbeque sauce, the smokiness from the smoked chicken and the sharpness from the blue cheese make this pizza absolutely delicious. If you don't like blue cheese, use mozzarella (however, I think you'll love it after trying this).

Ingredients

1 large wholewheat tortilla
2 tablespoons barbeque sauce
1 smoked chicken breast, cubed
2 tablespoons cubed yellow bell pepper
crumbled blue cheese (use according to taste)

Method

1. Preheat oven at 220°C.
2. Place the tortilla on a baking pan, spread the barbeque sauce, chicken, bell pepper and then the cheese evenly.
3. Bake for 12–14 minutes or until the crust is golden.

SUN-DRIED TOMATO PESTO AND MOZZARELLA PIZZA

Makes: 1

The key ingredient in this pizza is the sun-dried tomato pesto (can be found in supermarkets), which has a very subtle taste. Also try to use fresh bocconcini or mozzarella for this.

Ingredients

1 large wholewheat tortilla
2 tablespoons sun-dried tomato pesto
3 cloves of garlic, finely chopped
2 chicken ham slices or 5 salami, sliced
½–¾ cup of grated bocconcini mozzarella

Method

1. Preheat oven at 220°C.
2. Put the tortilla on a baking tray, spread the sauce, and evenly spread the toppings, sprinkling with the cheese.
3. Bake for 12–14 minutes or until the crust is golden.

CORN WITH FETA

Makes: 2

Corn on the cob! This can be eaten as a side to any of the mains or as a perfect after school/work snack. Delicious and healthy with a little twist. This hits all the notes–sweet, spicy, salty and crunchy!

Ingredients

2 golden half-steamed corn on the cob
½ tablespoon butter
2 tablespoons feta cheese
1 tablespoon finely chopped parsley
salt to taste
juice of a lemon

Method

1. Heat oven at 175°C.
2. Brush the half-steamed corn with butter and cook it in the oven for 10 minutes.
3. Mix the feta, parsley, seasoning and lemon juice in a bowl and pour on the cob.
4. The yummiest, most fulfilling cheesy herbed cob ready!

BAKED SWEET POTATO WEDGES

Makes: 3–4 portions

This makes a wonderful after-school/work snack. Sweet potatoes are complex carbohydrates which provide the body with energy and a lot of vitamins as well. I personally enjoy the taste of these more than original fries—these are sweet, salty, spicy and crispy all at the same time. Also, much healthier than French fries as these are baked instead of fried, but still just as satisfying. Although these do take 30 minutes to prepare, it is worth it as it saves on calories due to baking. To prevent sticking, I would recommend using baking or butter paper with the baking sheet, and spreading them out evenly to ensure crispiness.

Ingredients

2 medium-sized sweet potatoes
1 teaspoon salt
1 teaspoon cayenne pepper
1 teaspoon cinnamon powder
2 tablespoons olive oil

Method

1. Preheat oven at 220°C.
2. Wash and peel the sweet potatoes, and cut them into wedges.
3. Transfer the wedges into a bowl or a ziplock bag. Sprinkle with salt, cayenne pepper, cinnamon powder and olive all. Toss it all to mix well.
4. Spread on a baking tray with the butter paper and bake for 15 minutes. Flip the fries and bake for another 15 minutes.

CHEF'S TIP

You may half-boil the sweet potatoes before baking them as they cut short on the baking time.

FETA CUCUMBER

Makes: 1 portion

A quick and tasty snack that makes the boring cucumber so much more interesting. I sometimes eat this to balance my daily calories when I've had a very heavy lunch. The crunch of the chilled cucumber and walnuts go perfectly with the salty, creamy feta—a perfect alternative to unhealthy crackers and cheese.

Ingredients

2 tablespoons hung curd
2 tablespoons feta cheese
1 teaspoon lemon juice
2 cloves of garlic, crushed
½ a teaspoon honey
salt and pepper to taste (be careful with the salt as feta is a little salty)
1 large cucumber, cut lengthwise in half
walnuts for garnishing, chopped roughly

Method

5. In a small bowl, whisk well the curd, feta, lemon juice, garlic, honey and seasoning. Keep in the fridge, covered with a cling film.
6. Deseed the cucumber by scooping out the seeds.
7. Fill in the cavity of the cucumber with the cheese mix and garnish with chopped walnuts and eat!

DESSERTS AND DRINKS

Desserts! Too much! Too yum! But if you have to indulge your sweet tooth, you just have to! So what I worked out was the PORTIONS! I usually make my cake and eat it all too, literally! Of course, coconut oil, maple syrup, raw honey in desserts help cut down on the non-healthy ingredients, but I'm a little fussy about compromising too much on my taste. By the way, healthy doesn't necessarily mean low-fat/low-calories. But it's okay to indulge once in a while as long as we learn to control the portions. We all know that a single can of soda contains the equivalent of 10 teaspoons of sugar. Drinking soda regularly causes plaque to build up on the teeth and can lead to cavities and gum disease, cancer, obesity, cholesterol—basically as bad as it can get! Why not try something easy and healthy? So, here I've also shared my favourite drinks where I've replaced sugar with raw honey—the all-natural energy drink and sweet as hell! Yes, not low in calories, but super healthy!

patisse

CUPCAKES

Makes: 12 cupcakes

I've been making cupcakes since the last 4 years and have tried at least a dozen different recipes. But this recipe is, by far, the best I have ever had. The cupcakes are super moist, tender and won't crumble too much. The secret is to use oil instead of butter. Also, it is just a one-bowl recipe and involves no creaming or whipping! Using different frostings can easily flavour cupcakes and here I provide some of my favourites.

Ingredients

Master cupcake batter

1 cup castor sugar
⅓ cup coconut oil
1 egg
½ cup almond milk
¼ cup hot water
1 cup flour
pinch of salt
½ teaspoon vinegar
1 teaspoon baking powder
1 teaspoon vanilla essence

Whisk all the ingredients together in a bowl and keep aside

Cream cheese frosting

½ cup cream cheese (soft)
¼ cup butter
½ cup icing sugar

Whisk all the ingredients together in a bowl and keep aside

Buttercream frosting

⅓ cup soft butter
1 cup icing sugar
¼ cup milk
½ vanilla pod (only seeds) or a dash of vanilla extract

Whisk all the ingredients together in a bowl and keep aside

VANILLA BEAN CUPCAKES

Ingredients

Master cupcake batter
Buttercream frosting

Method

1. Preheat the oven at 165°C.
2. Transfer the batter to a greased muffin tin and bake for 20 minutes.
3. Pipe or spoon the frosting on the cooled cupcakes.

RED VELVET CUPCAKE

Ingredients

Master cupcake batter
1 tablespoon cocoa powder
dash of bottled red food colouring
Cream cheese frosting

Method

1. Preheat the oven at 165°C.
2. Add the cocoa powder and food colour to the cupcake batter and mix well.
3. Transfer the batter to a greased muffin tin and bake for 20 minutes.
4. Pipe the frosting on the cooled cupcakes.

MIXED BERRY CUPCAKE

Ingredients

Master cupcake batter
Buttercream frosting
¼ cup pureed mixed berry (strawberry, blueberry, raspberry. Berry yummy!)

Method

1. Preheat the oven at 165°C.
2. Transfer the batter to a greased muffin tin and bake for 20 minutes.
3. To make the frosting, just mix the pureed berries to the buttercream frosting and whisk it all together.
4. Pipe the frosting on the cooled cupcakes.

COCONUT LEMON CUPCAKE

Ingredients

Master cupcake batter
1 tablespoon lemon zest
1 teaspoon lemon juice
Buttercream frosting
⅓ cup coconut powder (desiccated)

Method

1. Preheat the oven at 165°C.
2. Add the lemon zest and juice to the cupcake batter and mix well.
3. Transfer the batter to a greased muffin tin and bake for 20 minutes.
4. In the meanwhile, whisk in the coconut powder with the buttercream frosting until light and fluffy.
5. Pipe the frosting on the cooled cupcakes.

DARK CHOCOLATE CUPCAKE

Ingredients

Master cupcake batter

⅓ cup cocoa powder

1 cup dark chocolate, melted in the microwave

Cream cheese frosting

½ cup icing sugar

¼ cup cocoa powder

Method

1. Preheat the oven at 165°C.
2. Add the cocoa powder and ½ cup of the melted dark chocolate to the cupcake batter and mix well.
3. Transfer the batter to a greased muffin tin and bake for 20 minutes.
4. For the frosting, whisk the icing sugar and cocoa powder with the cream cheese frosting prepared beforehand until light and fluffy.
5. Pipe the frosting on the cooled cupcakes.

CARROT AND WALNUT CUPCAKE

Ingredients

Master cupcake batter

1 teaspoon cinnamon powder

¾ cup grated carrots

Cream cheese frosting

Method

1. Preheat the oven at 165°C.
2. Add the cinnamon powder and grated carrots to the cupcake batter and mix well.
3. Transfer the batter to a greased muffin tin and bake for 20 minutes.
4. Pipe the frosting on the cooled cupcakes.

CHOCOLATE PUDDING

Makes: A 9-inch cake pan

Same old chocolate cake with a bang! Best served straight out of the oven with a scoop of cold vanilla ice cream, you are sure to love this easy, quick dessert. It is best to use a large rectangular baking dish or cake pan for this.

Ingredients

Cake

1 cup flour
¼ cup cocoa powder
½ cup brown sugar
½ cup milk
¼ cup coconut oil
1 egg
pinch of salt

Sauce

1½ cup boiling water
½ cup brown sugar
⅓ cup cocoa powder

Method

1. Preheat oven at 180°C.
2. In a bowl, simply whisk the flour, cocoa, sugar, milk, oil, egg and salt.
3. In another bowl, mix the water, sugar and cocoa.
4. Pour the cake mix into a greased cake pan and spread evenly. Pour the liquid mix on top and bake for 50 minutes.
5. Let it rest for at least 10 minutes and serve with vanilla ice cream (optional).

ULTIMATE CHEESECAKE

Makes: 6–8 portions, depends how greedy you are!

No matter what part of the world I visit, I try to sample as many cheesecakes as I can. Therefore I consider myself as the "master of cheesecakes". Unfortunately, my favourite dessert is also a bomb of calories—around 800 calories in just a slice. But don't worry, you can now enjoy this treat without the guilt because I've found a way to reduce the calories by more than half! The secret ingredient—Quark/ Kwark cheese. Although this is so much lower in fat and calories, I guarantee that it will satisfiy you as much as the original. The raspberry compote takes the already delicious cheesecake to a newer level.

Ingredients

Base

1½ cup crushed digestive biscuits (I put the biscuits in a ziplock and beat them up)
⅓ cup butter, melted

Filling

2 cups Kwark
½ cup castor sugar
1 lemon (zest and juice)
dash of vanilla essence
2 tablespoons flour
4 eggs

Compote

1 cup berries (raspberry or blueberry)
½ cup raw honey

Method

1. Preheat the oven at 160°C.
2. To prepare the base, mix the crushed biscuits with the butter.
3. Press this mix tightly in a loose bottom cake pan with a spoon. Chill in the fridge for an hour.
4. Mix all the ingredients for the filling. Pour on top of the base and bake for 40–45 minutes.
5. To prepare the compote, just bring the berries and honey to a simmer in a pan for about 5 minutes.
6. The cheesecake MUST be chilled for at least 4 hours in the fridge. For best results, overnight.
7. Serve chilled, topped with the berry compote.

CLASSIC CHEESECAKE

Makes: 4 ramekins or a 6-inch cake pan

A cheesecake is literally a blank canvas, it can be served with berries, chocolate, caramel or just plain; probably why it's my favourite dessert. Unfortunately, it is also comes with a lot of calories. But don't worry, now you can enjoy this treat without the guilt, but in small portions. This cheesecake, however, offers a twist in the recipe with the use of coconut cream!

Ingredients

Base

6 large digestive biscuits
2 tablespoons water

Filling

1 cup cream cheese
½ cup coconut cream
½ cup icing sugar
1 teaspoon vanilla essence
2 eggs

Compote (optional)

½ cup frozen or fresh raspberries
2 tablespoons raw honey
1 teaspoon water

Method

1. Preheat the oven at 150°C.
2. To prepare the base, microwave the biscuits and water for 30 seconds.
3. Mix the biscuits until they come together and press in the ramekins or cake pan.
4. Mix all the ingredients for the filling in a bowl. Pour on top of the base and bake for 40 minutes.
5. To prepare the compote, just bring the berries, honey and water to a simmer in a pan for about 5 minutes or microwave for 3 minutes.
6. The cheesecake MUST be chilled for at least 6 hours in the fridge. For best results, overnight. Then top with the compote and dig in!

TIRAMISU

Makes: 3 portions

The classic Tiramisu, no variations! Made just the way it was intended—mascarpone, egg whites and savoiardi cookies. Make these for a dinner party and your guests will go bonkers.

Ingredients

1½ cup mascarpone cheese
⅔ cup castor sugar
3 eggs, separated
18 sponge lady finger biscuits (savoiardi, halved or cat's tongue biscuits)
1 cup strong black coffee
cocoa powder for dusting

Method

1. In a bowl, whisk together the cheese, sugar and egg yolks.
2. In another bowl, whip the egg whites to stiff peaks. Fold into the cheese mix.
3. Dip the biscuits in the coffee.
4. In a martini glass, place two biscuits and then layer with the cheese mix.
5. Make 3 layers of the biscuits and cheese mix with the cream on top.
6. Leave it to chill in the refrigerator for an hour or more to let it set.
7. Dust with the cocoa powder and serve.

Brasil

Chocolate Chip Cookie Pie

Makes: A 9-inch cake pan

A large chewy, soft cookie, this is absolutely delicious. Inspired by the skillet cookie (the same but just baked in a skillet) this "pie" is actually a mix between a brownie and a cookie—two of my favourite desserts. This is an easy recipe and I think it is impossible to go wrong with this—an absolute crowd pleaser, a perfect dessert for when friends come over. The gooey, chocolaty centre of a cookie is what I like best. So a larger cookie ensures more of the centre.

The secret behind the chewiness of a cookie is the molasses present in brown sugar, therefore it cannot be substituted entirely by regular sugar. The batter is softer than a traditional cookie dough, more like that of a Victoria sponge cake. This dessert can be made in 20 minutes flat, unlike a cake, and the best part is that it's supposed to be served warm, so no need to wait for it to cool.

Ingredients

¾ cups butter
⅓ cup brown sugar
½ cup castor sugar
1 egg
1 cup flour
pinch of salt
¾ cup dark chocolate chunks (roughly cut)

Method

1. Preheat oven at 175°C.
2. Melt butter in a microwave, add the brown sugar and castor sugar to it and mix well.
3. Mix in the egg, flour and salt.
4. Stir in the chocolate chunks.
5. Bake in a greased round non-stick cake pan for 18 minutes.
6. Let it cool slightly for 5 minutes and slice, or just dig in.

CHEAT FRENCH CHOCO CAKE

Makes: 4 ramekins or a 9-inch cake pan

A French chocolate cake, which I consider to be my favourite kind of chocolate cake, is extremely heavy. Though my recipe is a cheat, it is dense, chocolaty, light and super moist, more like a baked mousse than a cake. What makes it the "best" is the fact that it has only ¼ of the calories of the original version. I use a very small amount of chocolate and cocoa powder. Also, it literally has no butter, making it a low-calorie, guilt-free dessert. However, this cake tastes rich, decadent and delicious. EVERYONE MUST TRY THIS!

Ingredients

cooking spray
2 tablespoons flour
⅔ cup castor sugar
pinch of salt
1 cup milk
1 cup dark chocolate
⅓ cup cocoa powder
2 egg yolks
3 egg whites
¼ cup castor sugar

Method

1. Preheat oven at 175°C. Line a 9-inch round cake pan with foil or baking paper in the bottom.
2. In a saucepan, add flour, castor sugar, salt and ¼ cup milk. Mix these to make a lump-free paste. Slowly add the rest of the milk.
3. Cook this mix for 2–3 minutes, stirring until the mixture thickens. Remove from heat and add the chocolate, cocoa and mix until the residual heat melts all the chocolate.
4. Let this cool for 5 minutes and then add the yolks.
5. In a bowl, beat egg whites to stiff peaks. Add the sugar gradually.

6. Fold the egg whites gently into the cooled chocolate mix. Pour into the cake tin.
7. Take a larger pan or dish and fill halfway with boiling water. Cover the base of the cake tin with foil and place in the larger pan. This is known as a "water bath". Bake for 25 minutes.
8. After taking it out from the oven, let it rest for at least 30 minutes and then remove from the pan.
9. Dust with icing sugar and serve.

COCONUT AND RASPBERRY BAKEWELL CAKE

Makes: A 9-inch cake pan

The traditional Bakewell tart is my favourite kind of tart, but combining it with coconut and raspberry flavours makes it even better. Plus we save a lot of calories by avoiding the short crust pastry—still just as good.

Ingredients

⅔ cup coconut oil
2 cups ground almonds (or almond flour)
1¼ cup flour
¾ cup castor sugar
3 eggs
½ cup raspberries (fresh or frozen)
almond flakes
icing sugar

Method

1. Preheat oven at 180°C.
2. In a bowl, whisk the oil, ground almonds, flour, sugar and eggs.
3. In a greased tin, put half of this cake mixture. Scatter the mix with enough raspberries. Cover the tin with the rest of the batter.
4. Now sprinkle with the flaked almonds.
5. Bake for 40–45 minutes or until golden.
6. Serve warm with a sprinkle of icing sugar.

CHEAT PINEAPPLE UPSIDE DOWN

Makes: 4 portions

In the mood for a yummy pineapple dessert, but feeling lazy? I've got the perfect recipe for you. This "cake" is made of regular burger buns, but is just as tasty as the cake, therefore, no compromises. This might take as much baking time as a regular cake, but takes almost no effort to make.

Ingredients

¼ cup butter
⅔ cup brown sugar
2 burger buns
4 pineapple slices (fresh)

Method

1. Preheat oven at 175°C.
2. Melt the butter in a pan, add brown sugar and keep stirring for 2–3 minutes on a low flame or until dissolved.
3. Slice the buns in half to make 4 pieces. Place the buns on a greased baking dish, cut side up.
4. Place a pineapple piece on each bun and cover with the brown sugar mix.
5. Bake for 25 minutes, and serve piping hot with a scoop of vanilla ice cream.

COCOA FUDGE COOKIES

Makes: 6 cookies

Much lower in calories than regular fudge cookies, my recipe produces a fudgy, chewy and crisp cookie that always satisfies my cookie cravings on cheat days.

Ingredients

⅓ cup cocoa powder
⅓ cup butter, melted
⅔ cup castor sugar
⅓ cup brown sugar
⅓ cup yoghurt or 1 egg
1 cup flour
½ tablespoon baking soda
dash of vanilla essence

Method

1. Preheat oven at 175°C.
2. Mix the cocoa powder, butter and sugar together.
3. Add the yoghurt or one egg and fold the ingredients together so as to keep it light and fluffy.
4. Add all the flour and then the baking soda to combine to form a dry cookie dough.
5. Take small balls of the dough and flatten into thin discs using your hands.
6. Place on a greased baking tray at least 2 inches apart and bake for 9 minutes.
7. Before removing from the tray, let the cookies set for at least 30 minutes.

OREO MILKSHAKE

Makes: 1 glass

Oreo milkshake is my all-time favourite milkshake. It's super thick, chilled and extremely refreshing. A perfect drink for hot summer days which also acts as a dessert (yes, it's that tasty). The secret to any good milkshake in general is a thick consistency, which can only be achieved by using sufficient amount of ice cream—about 3 large scoops per glass. To make this healthy, I use oats as a thickening agent.

Ingredients

1 scoop vanilla/chocolate ice cream
¾ cup almond milk
¼ cup quick oats
1 tablespoon drinking chocolate (optional)
7 Oreo cookies

Method

Blend all these ingredients in a blender or by using a hand blender and serve chilled.

KIWI FIZZ

Makes: 1 tall glass

An excellent source of Vitamin C, Kiwi is one of my favourite fruit. The beautiful green colour of this drink not only makes it the most inviting summer drink, but also the most delicious. Kiwi is undoubtedly the perfect fruit for a drink, desert or salad!

Ingredients

2 medium-sized kiwi, peeled and pureed with a fork
juice of a lemon
2 tablespoons raw honey
chilled soda (fill the glass)

Method

Simply blend all the ingredients and serve chilled.

LEMON MINT SODA

Makes: 1 tall glass

Love store-bought sodas? If yes, then you should know that they contain a ton of artificial sugars and unhealthy ingredients. Well, you can make it at home without compromising on the taste and flavour. Refreshing and tasty, this is going to give you a kick of instant energy.

Ingredients

½ a lemon, cut into small cubes
handful of mint leaves
2 tablespoons honey
chilled soda (fill it up)

Method

1. In a glass, put the lemons and mint. With a spoon/fork crush this mix until the juices are released. Add the honey.
2. Fill up the glass with soda.
3. Stir. Serve!

RASPBERRY SODA

Makes: 1 tall glass

I don't know whether traditional or not, but raspberry soda is the drink of my choice at my favourite Parsi restaurant. I love the fact that almost every sip contains a mouthful of raspberry puree.

Ingredients

½ glass frozen or fresh raspberry
2 tablespoons raw honey
juice of a lemon
cold soda (fill it up)

Method

1. Fill the raspberries in the glass, along with the honey and lemon juice. Crush with a spoon/fork.
2. Add the chilled soda, stir and serve.

MEXICAN CHIA FRESCA

Makes: 1 tall glass

A wonderful way to incorporate chia seeds into your daily diet. This drink is apparently very popular in Mexico and other South American countries. Chia seeds are packed with nutrients, antioxidants, fibre and protein. When soaked in water, they swell up and the texture is pretty good.

Ingredients

½ tablespoon chia seeds
juice of two medium-sized lemons
2 tablespoons raw honey
chilled water (fill up the glass)

Method

1. In a glass, stir in all the ingredients.
2. Let it rest in the fridge for at least 20 minutes so the chia seeds swell up and then serve.

TADKA CHHAS

Makes: 1 tall glass

A perfect summer drink made with butter milk—quick, super healthy and, of course, delicious. An amazing digestive.

Ingredients

½ teaspoon any oil
¼ teaspoon mustard seeds
6 curry leaves
½ teaspoon roasted cumin powder
salt to taste
1 glass chilled butter milk

Method

1. In a pan, heat the oil, add the mustard seeds and as they start to pop, throw in the curry leaves and leave it on the flame till nice and crisp.
2. Stir in the salt and cumin powder to the cold glass of butter milk.
3. Top it with the tadka and serve.

ALMOND MILK THANDAI

Makes: 1 large jar or 4 glasses

A cool, rich and decadent beverage, the drink of champions! Loaded with spices, nuts, chia and oats, this makes the perfect breakfast on the go, as it can be made a night before. Instead of regular milk I use almond milk to cut down on the calories. For a coconut twist use a cup of coconut milk (optional).

Ingredients

4 cups almond milk (or 3 cups+1 cup coconut milk)
½ cup almonds, soaked and blanched
¼ cup cashews
½ cup honey
1 teaspoon cinnamon
4 black peppercorns
4 pods of cardamom
1 tablespoon chia seeds
¼ cup oats
2 tablespoons fennel seeds
handful of mint leaves
pinch of saffron

Method

1. In a blender, add all the ingredients except for the saffron with only 1 cup of milk. Blend for 3–4 minutes or until super smooth.
2. In a saucepan, heat the rest of the milk and add the saffron. Let it infuse on medium heat for a minute and add the nut spice mix. Stir for 3–4 minutes or until all flavours mingle.
3. Transfer to a jug or a few glasses and refrigerate overnight for best results. Serve chilled.

INSPIRE

Reflect! Motivate! Energise!

Filmstars, sportsperson and chefs! Fitness gurus and celebrities did not blink an eyelid before replying to all my mails, and contributing to the richness of my book—that too for someone they hardly knew! I have put in a lot of research into the making of the questionaire, keeping in mind their specific interest and background. These celebrities share their food habits, their fitness regime, some health tips and their favourite recipes. Questions every youngster has in mind, now answered!

Courtsey: John Abraham

JOHN ABRAHAM Model & Actor

When did your interest in fitness begin?

My interest in fitness began at the age of 15.

Do you cook?

I do not cook.

What is your favourite cuisine and dish?

Parsi food. I love *patrani macchi*.

Do you prefer savoury food or desserts?

Neither.

What kind of foods do you consume on a daily basis?

Salads, egg whites, oats.

What is the best way for an overweight teenager to lose weight, and can he/she use supplements such as fat burners or powders?

Just play a sport till you're 21. Concentrating on a healthy diet and a good exercise routine and good rest is good enough to lose weight. Fat burners are no good. Whey Proteins are good only if you work out on a regular basis.

How do you stick to your diet? Don't you get demotivated at times and have cravings like the rest of us?

Getting demotivated is meant for the weak. You have to be strong. This is Sparta!

How often do you cheat on your diet?

I believe in a consistent healthy lifestyle. Cheating is for the weak.

Could you give some tips to teens who aspire to have a well-sculpted fit body such as yours?

Think clean. Live clean. Sleep clean and work out like a beast.

Lastly, if possible can you please provide an easy-to-make recipe that you consider healthy?

Go and boil some eggs and have the whites. Easy to do, easy to consume.

MILIND SOMAN Model & Actor

What was your favourite thing to eat as a child? Were you fond of Scottish food?

Bananas. I love eating fish and meat.

How do you look so young? Just good genes? What's your biggest secret?

Since childhood, I used to swim intensively, spending 3–5 hours in the pool, training 5 days a week. And yes, genes also play some role but focus and dedication is very important.

How did your interest in fitness begin?

I started swimming at the age of 10. The same year, I won a silver medal at the national championship and my journey with fitness continued.

Personally, even running 5 km for a few days, bores me out. You probably run 10 times more than me, so how do you keep yourself motivated? Don't you get bored?

For me, fitness is liberating. The people who don't do this don't understand the tremendous high endurance sports gives you. When that happens, there is no pain. It's just bliss.

Tell us about your Ironman journey. How did you train yourself?

Training for a race like Ironman requires your entire being and all your energies—physical, mental, emotional and spiritual—to come together. It's just a bliss, not a pain. I was invited by a friend Lihas Trivedi, who organised a Triathlon in Ahmedabad, to give away the prizes. There I met the Director of the event, Kimberly Shah, an American professional athlete. She asked me to try Ironman and offered to train me for it and sent

Courtsey: Milind Soman

me a plan. It involved 35 hours of training a week for 3–4 months. It has marked a lifestyle change for me.

What is your basic fitness regime? Do you include weight training? I've heard that just running without weight conditioning can harm you in the long run.

I don't go to the gym. I try running at least twice a week.

Do you follow a diet? What does a typical diet consist of? Do you stay away from any particular food?

I have never followed a diet. The only thing I avoid is refined sugar. I love eating fish and meat. We Maharashtrians eat a lot of ghee and butter and I love the taste of ghee; I, practically, have it with every meal.

Any tips for teenagers who want to be healthy?

My advice for teenagers would be to take it slow and easy. Be patient with yourself. Explore your body's responses. Learn to listen to your body.
It can be tricky for the body to get comfortable with that kind of intense effort. Endurance sport teaches us one thing—if you work at something you love, patiently, consistently and with focus, not only will you get where you want to get, but every moment you will be where you want to be.

Courtsey: R Madhavan

R MADHAVAN Actor

As a child, what was your favourite food?

My favourite food was South Indian curd rice—an all-time comfort food. For "fast food" I loved (and still love) pani puri and aloo chat.

Where you always interested in fitness?

No, not always, my interest began when I joined the National Cadet Corps.

Everyone with an amazing body has their own secret. What's your one secret to good health?

My secret to good health is not feeling guilty about what I eat, respecting my body and living a stress-free life.

What do you think is the best way for an overweight person to lose weight?

The first thing for an overweight person is to have the desire to lose weight, how to do it won't be a problem as there are a million people to help. But the most important thing is to have it in the bottom of your heart and then work towards it—one small step at a time.

Do you follow a strict daily diet to maintain your physique?

No, I do not. As I travel a lot, I don't necessarily get the "ideal diet" on a daily basis. But I don't eat what makes me feel guilty. I try to chew 40 times and taste every morsel that I put into my mouth. Also, I make it a point to not overeat.

How do you stick to your diet, don't you get demotivated at times and have cravings like the rest of us?

According to me, the worst thing you can do is go on a strict diet to lose weight as quick as possible, because whatever you lose will come back twice as much due to the stress of dieting. It needs to come from within, and as I said earlier—one step at a time.

What does your fitness regime look like?

For my film *Saala Khadoos*, I put on a lot of muscle as I played a retired boxer, working out for exactly 45 minutes a day. But I really took my time to transform my body—11 months, 4 times a week and 1 day of light cardio.

Do you prefer savoury food or desserts?

I go through this phase of preferring both, just depending on what my body is craving. But whatever I eat, I make sure to chew it, taste it and once I'm satisfied, I don't overeat.

What is your favourite cuisine and dish (can be from home or a restaurant). Are you a fan of junk food such as pizzas and burgers?

I think that everyone becomes a fan of junk food at one point in their life; it's important to indulge. My trainer once told me, that you should fully indulge on a Sunday, and really go overboard with it (have a whole pizza if you want)—this is so you don't crave it the rest of the week and so your body goes into a shock, not absorbing all the fat.

How often do you cheat on your diet? If you could eat a meal without gaining any calories, what would it consist of (i.e., ultimate cheat meal)?

There's not really a scope of cheating on my diet, as I eat whatever I get. The most important part is to focus when eating—you don't talk, text or use your phone, no TV either. Those 15 minutes are yours to nourish the body. While watching TV, one tends to overeat too, which could give rise to dreaded "love handles (side fat)".

Lastly, could you please provide an easy-to-make recipe that you like?

My favourite snack is a chapatti (roti) with a thin omelette rolled inside. I just eat it with a bit of salt and chaat masala.

TIGER SHROFF Actor

You are apparently one of the most dedicated, disciplined fitness freaks in Bollywood. What motivates you to work out seven times a week? Don't you ever feel lazy and not wanting to work out?

Thankfully, I've been into fitness ever since I can remember. I started martial arts at the age of 5, and have always been an athlete in school, etc. Fitness is simply a part of my life and is not something I do because I "have" to! So to answer your question, it's what I love to do.

When did you discover fitness in your life?

I've always been active! Like I said, I've been into martial arts since I was 5 and I think I've been swimming since I was 6 months old probably! Weight training is something I got into when I was around 15 years.

How much time did it take you to achieve your current ripped physique?

Right until *Heropanti*, I was pretty beefy and heavy, around 85 kg. I realised that on-screen I'd look even bigger, so I completely changed my diet and workout pattern and came down to around 75 kg of lean muscle. Now I work out to maintain this physique, which I feel is ideal for the screen.

Since you are into martial arts too, would you prefer a strength-trying workout outdoors or an iron-pumping indoor gym workout?

I love all my workouts! Be it gymnastics, or martial arts, or weight training, or even just a great game of football or basketball with friends. Anything that gets you moving and your blood pumping is great.

Are you a foodie? How important do you think food is in contributing to your physique?

I'm a huge foodie! I could eat a horse if I could! So for me, the diet part of

Courtsey: Tiger Shroff

my regime is the hardest. I would say my diet contributes 80% to the way my body looks at any given time.

Do you cook? If yes, then what is the best dish you can make?

I can't cook at all! But if I did, it would probably be some amazing dessert! My favourite is peanut butter and Nutella sandwiches!

What is your ultimate favourite food (can be from a restaurant or from your home). Also, do you believe in cheat days? If yes, what does your ultimate cheat meal consist of?

Like I said, I've got a crazy sweet tooth and desserts is what I crave the most! Indigo Cafe makes the most amazing peanut butter and Nutella sandwiches and that's what I indulge in on cheat days. Cheat days are vital to your diet plan in order to keep your body from getting too efficient in terms of calorie savings and therefore you would end up burning less fat actually. The trick is to go with protein and fibre meals regularly and then once a week get in some fats. But again, timing is vital and I would normally have a cheat meal after a heavy workout like legs, for example.

Many people including some doctors and trainers say that bodybuilding to lose weight will stunt a teenager's growth and therefore should be avoided until the age of 21? Do you agree?

There are many opinions surrounding exercise and diet. You must find what works best for you. Like I mentioned earlier, I started weight training at the age of 15.

Can you please give a few key tips to teens who aspire to have a body such as yours?

The biggest tip I can share is discipline. If you are disciplined, you can achieve anything you set your mind to. Clean living, clean thinking, clean eating on a consistent basis will get you results, and trust me, there's no better feeling than to be full of energy and live healthy!

Lastly, could you please provide a healthy simple recipe that you consume, and you can cook yourself (or not)?

Well, this is something I get at home and it's healthy as well as tasty! Take around 200 g of Scottish salmon fillet and marinate it in a mixture of paprika, black pepper, sea salt, garlic, lemon juice, oregano, thyme, and olive oil (use quantities as per your personal taste, like for example, I don't like too much garlic). Preheat your oven to about 250°C and bake your fish for about 10–15 minutes till it's cooked to your liking. I usually eat this with a side of steamed broccoli or roasted sweet potatoes. It's super healthy and super tasty!

GAGANJEET BHULLAR Golfer

What was your favourite food as a child?

Like any other kid from Punjab, butter chicken was my favourite. Now it's a thing of the past. Whenever I smell it, I do get very tempted but I know I have to avoid it to remain fit.

Golfers don't seem to be running as much as, say, footballers. How important is fitness in a sport such as golf?

Fitness is extremely important for us golfers since most of us spend almost 45 weeks a year on tour. What makes it even more difficult is that we are at different locations every other week. Sometimes the time zones vary drastically. For example, this week we play in Switzerland and the next in Hong Kong. Staying fit is the only solution.

What does your daily diet consist of? How particular are you about your diet?

As the fitness pundits say, breakfast is the most important meal and it truly is. I have a heavy breakfast. Besides that I have 5 other smaller meals during the day which does not leave me too hungry and gives me the energy to last the day on the golf course. My diet is a mix of protein, carbohydrates and iron. I personally believe that a mixed diet is better than just one particular type.

How often do you work out? What does a workout consist of?

Due to our hectic travel schedule, the first thing I usually do when I check into a hotel is hit the gym for 80 minutes at a go. This mainly consists of cycling for 45 minutes (cardio), 15 minutes of stretching, which is very important for golfers, and finally 20 minutes of core exercise.

Courtsey: Varun Menon

Do you have any cheat days? If you could eat whatever you wanted without gaining any calories, what would your ultimate cheat meal consist of?

No cheat days. I think the whole purpose of working out is defeated with a cheat day. Although I sometimes do indulge in a bit of eating "something nice". Banana splits is my favourite along with a good hamburger. To be very honest, this happens maybe once or maximum twice a year. But when I do have it, I really savour it.

What is your most favourite dish (can be from any restaurant or home)?

Well I love Thai food. The EEST at the Westin Hotels and Resorts is one of my favourite restaurants for good Oriental cuisine. Home food is always where the heart is, since I travel so much. Nothing beats the good old aloo parantha and lassi.

A game of golf lasts for a long period of time. Do you eat anything before a game, to get energy?

If it is a morning tee off, my morning breakfast is more than sufficient to help me last. However, I always carry bananas and apples in my golf bag to give me energy and keep me fuelled for the round. Water is absolutely essential. I avoid any form of aerated drinks.

Lastly, could you please provide an easy recipe of something that you love to eat?

The egg white omelette. It's simple. And one cannot really ruin it. I try and add mushrooms, tomatoes, a little bit of chilli and maybe some bacon for a bite. Can't think of a day when I can go without breakfast without an omelette.

Interview courtesy: Varun Menon, RN Golf Management Pvt.Ltd

KRISHAN TIWARI Fitness Trainer

When did your interest in fitness begin?

When I started playing football in school—Class 8.

What does your daily diet consist of? What is your favourite thing to eat in general (can be from a restaurant or home)?

Breakfast, usually a glass of coconut water, oats porridge with lots of vegetables. A glass of milk around noon. For lunch, a bowl of salad, green vegetables, a bowl of boiled rice and fish (3 times a week). Evening, one fruit. Dinner, 6 boiled eggs and steamed vegetables. Favourite food, grilled fish.

What are your views on "cheat meals"? How often can they be had?

I believe it is important to treat yourself with a cheat meal once a month.

If you could eat anything you wanted without gaining any calories, what would you eat?

Kheer.

Many trainers and doctors have told me that I should not even think about weight training till the age of 18 or 21. Is it okay for a teenager to do bodybuilding?

Before 18 it is better to do only body weight resistance training. There are different ways of training every body part for strength. It is a myth that you need extra weight for muscular development, Calisthenics and body weight training is just as effective.

What is a perfect teenager's diet?

A balanced diet with lots of fruits, healthy carbs like boiled potatoes, wholegrain breads and rotis; lean proteins like fish, eggs, beans; and dairy products like milk and curd. Avoid fried foods.

To lose weight, how many hours and days should a teenager work out?

These days a teenager's lifestyle is very sedentary. Between studies, TV, Internet and video games, physical activity is very limited, so it is important to work out and play outdoors for at least 2 hours a day. Workout can be every day since there is very little physical activity otherwise.

Is running a better option than weight training for weight loss?

There is no better or worse method to lose weight. Whether running or weight training, it all depends on the intensity and variety in method of workout.

Is it safe for a teenager to use supplements like whey protein?

Whey protein is safe but not required unless there is a lack in diet, or low B12 and D3 levels. Even then, it is better to go for natural proteins like fish, eggs, etc.

What was your favourite thing to eat as a child?

Ice cream!

Could you please share any easy recipe that you like to eat?

Boiled chicken with lemon and black pepper.

MARY KOM Boxer

How did you start boxing?

I have always loved martial arts since my childhood. When women's boxing was introdced, I got attracted to it and thought it will suit me more than athletics.

What was your favourite food growing up?

No specific food. Used to like everything served.

Can you cook? What is your favourite food?

Yes, I am indeed a good cook. I love cooking and I always try to churn out new recipes of my own. No favourite as such but I just love our indigenous foods.

Being a mother and a boxing champion, how difficult is it to balance your workout and travel regime?

More than balancing, it is tiring and the most difficult part is being away from my kids. I am able to balance my workouts and travels with the help of my family members. Being a boxer, staying extremely fit is a necessity.

How often do you indulge in "cheat days"?

My case is very different. Once I start practising hard, my weight goes down drastically. I sometimes have to eat a lot to put on weight. So I don't have any specific cheat days.

Are you a foodie, do you like junk food?

Yes, I am. I do like junk food.

Courtsey: Onler Kom

While preparing for a competition, what does your diet consist of?

Nothing special. But I always make sure I have that special rice we have at home.

Any health tip you want to give to teenagers, as we are surrounded and spoilt for choice regarding all the international junk food so easily available now?

Exercises are not only for sportspersons. Please have a regular workout regime. Eat junk food just to taste them once in a while but remember they are not as healthy as they taste. Health is everything.

Can you please provide an easy and healthy recipe that you eat?

Stew: first boil water for soup/gravy, add some ginger, onion and chilli, now put the main item (any green veg), leave for 2 min, after that you can add desired amount of salt, dry fish/meat or tastemaker (optional). When almost cooked, add grinded garlic. Do not overcook the veg.

Interview courtesy: Vijay Dubey, IOS India

Courtsey: Live Images

SAINA NEHWAL Badminton Player

What was your favourite food when you were growing up?

I was a very poor eater till 10 years of age, eating only homemade food like wheat chapattis, daals, kidney bean, black urad, homemade sweets like kheer (rice and milk dessert), seasonal fruits, curd, milk, etc., and no tea till 10 years of age. Once in a month or even more rarely I'd eat food from outside just for taste not to eat as a meal. I also liked pani puri once in a while.

What does your daily diet consist of?

Once I went into badminton, my coaches guided me as to what to eat or what not. I like sprouts in the morning, with lots of milk, fresh fruit juice, etc., and no tea or sweets. I take small amounts of rice and chicken for lunch.

Do you believe in cheat meals or eating unhealthy food? What would your ultimate cheat meal consist of?

I have no idea about cheat food, I knew about junk food or fast food but nothing else. I like homemade food when home. On foreign tours I enjoy the breakfast spread in hotels, but for lunch and dinner I prefer Indian meals in the peace and quiet of my room.

So how often do you play badminton? How many hours does a session consist of?

6 days a week, 3 sessions of about 2 hours each, as prepared by my coaches as per the need of the badminton game I follow. It includes workout as well as practice, there is no separate workout session.

Do you include weight training in your workout? What does a typical workout consist of?

Yes, I do, but under the guidance of my trainers and coaches.

What is your favourite thing to eat at home or favourite restaurant to visit?

Kheer.

Do you play any other sport?

No, only badminton.

Many athletes consume something before going out for a game. Do you eat anything before playing a big match?

No, I do not take any food before my game.

Lastly, could you please provide an easy recipe that you eat often?

Nothing specific, only homemade food with a little touch of non-veg for lunch.

ANAHITA N DHONDY Chef

How and when did your experience with cooking start?

Since I was 10, I've been helping my mom ice cakes. And before I knew it, by the time I was 13, I found myself cooking in most of my free time that I got from school. By then I knew that I wanted to be a chef.

Growing up (as a child and teenager), what was your favourite cuisine and meal (can be from any restaurant as well)?

As children and teenagers most of us are fussy eaters, but I wasn't one. I would try everything and want to know more about it, even try and cook it! We did have evenings out but I remember being a crazy fan of ice cream, chocolates, everything sweet, which has died down a lot over the years.

When did you realise that you wanted to be a chef?

By the time I was 14, I was sure I wanted to be a chef.

Although you studied pastry at Le Cordon Bleu, you chose to specialise in Parsi cuisine. Why?

When I was studying in IHM Aurangabad, I was always more inclined towards pastry. But during my internships where I insisted on being in the bakery, my chef gave me some great advice saying, "You won't be a head chef if you only specialise in Pastry and Bakery" and that's what got me thinking about how I wanted to learn everything and not be stuck in one part of the culinary world. When I went to Le Cordon Bleu, I didn't only specialise in pastry but pursued the "Grande Diplome", which concentrates equally on both patisserie and cuisine. I found out that I was very good in the hot kitchen as well. That's when I started really enjoying cuisine, French especially. Parsi food is something which is from my home, from my

Courtsey: Anahita N Dhondy

heart, I use a lot of skills from French cuisine and what I've learnt about kitchen management from Le Cordon Bleu.

How do you stay so fit despite being surrounded by amazing food the whole day?

You'll always find me snacking in the kitchen. I did put on a few kilos in the initial years of training because when you first enter the kitchen you want to try EVERYTHING! So you'll always find interns/new joinees constantly sneaking and munching around but then you really get over it. It's only in the beginning that you get greedy when you're surrounded by food, but over the years you learn to eat little and that too things that you don't cook. I love eating regular *ghar ka khana*, I carry it with me to work. And otherwise, tasting all day keeps me fit.

What is your ultimate guilty pleasure and how often do you indulge yourself?

Well, I love chocolates, and ice cream, really juicy barbequed pork ribs and lots of wine! Chilled fresh fruits, soufflés and lots of TIRAMISU, I could have tubs of it!

Can you please provide a simple, quick recipe that you really love to eat?

Akoori and toast for supper. Thanks to these Parsi masala eggs, we can now say goodbye to the boring bland eggs that most of us are used to eating. The eggs are soft, creamy, spicy and pack a punch. Serve with a few slices of generously buttered toasts and it'll knock your socks off!

AKOORI

Ingredients

Eggs	3 is perfect, 4 is greedy
Oil	2 tbsp
Onion	2 medium-sized, chopped fine

Tomatoes	2 medium-sized, chopped fine
Garlic paste/chopped	½ tsp
Green chillies	1 slit and chopped fine (2 if you like it spicy like I do)
Parsi sambhar masala	1 tsp
Turmeric powder	½ tsp
Red chilli powder	½ tsp
Salt	to taste
Pepper	a sprinkle
Butter	1 tbsp
Fresh coriander	as much as you wish, I like loads of it
Bread	2 slices, slathered with butter (butter is good for you!)

Method

1. In a frying pan, add the oil, let it get hot. Add the garlic paste, green chillies and the onions and brown well.
2. Once brown, add the masalas and cook. Add the chopped tomatoes and keep cooking till the rawness dies out.
3. Add salt and pepper. Then add half of the coriander and cook till it's a nice red paste.
   Note: This masala can be cooked and cooled, and kept in your fridge. You can add paneer if you're a total vegetarian and don't even eat eggs.
4. Next, whisk up the eggs in a bowl, add a pinch of salt.
5. The addition of eggs is crucial as the pan has to be hot with the masala, and just a few mixes should be good. It must be soft and not hard like a *bhurji*, and beaten down well. Add the butter and lots of coriander. Check for seasoning.
6. Toast the bread, slather some butter and top with the soft, fluffy and creamy akoori.
7. Throw in some more coriander if you like.
8. Tuck into this velvety egg preparation while cozying up on your couch, reading your favourite novel after a long day at work. Easy, healthy (ignore that butter) and yummy.

Courtsey: Manish Mehrotra

MANISH MEHROTRA Chef

What drew you towards cooking? When did you start cooking?

I started cooking when I went for the hotel management course. Before that, I wasn't inspired by my mother or grandmother or something like that. Cooking felt very creative to me and that's what really drew me towards it.

As a child/teenager, what was your favourite food?

Growing up in a small town like Patna, where there weren't many fancy restaurants, my food habits weren't very adventurous at that point of time. I belonged to a "no onion, no garlic" family, but my parents never stopped me from eating outside the house. So, I would say, everything that was made at home and at restaurants occasionally.

It's no secret, that your food is pleasantly "different" from classic Indian food. Creating dishes like a Duck Cornetto or a Blue Cheese Naan would really need another level of genius. How did you come up with such crazy dishes?

I started with Indian Accent when I had gathered around 15 years of experience in the food world. So these were simply created with the knowledge I had, the travelling I had done, the restaurants I had eaten at and even inspired by our day-to-day life.

What is the secret of your immense knowledge of such international foods that are so rarely found on menus across India?

I read a lot, so I've got a great collection of books that I take reference from. I have also travelled a lot and eaten at some of the best restaurants across the world. All these experiences have contributed to my knowledge.

Tell us a bit more about the menu of the health club that you designed at The Manor. What kinds of ingredients do you use to make your food healthy? Can you give a few examples of healthy interesting dishes?

The image of "health foods" in India is quite different from what people usually think it is. When they think about healthy food, they think about sprouts, tofu, lettuce, salads and all these things. My aim was to create health foods in such a way, that it would be created with healthy ingredients but much more tasty, appetising and appealing to people. We use ingredients with are healthy alternatives to heavy foods. For example, the people of India love Biryani (a rice and meat dish), so we created a Lamb and Quinoa Biryani. We also do a gluten-free Uttapam Pizza, with less oil and absolutely no cheese.

Do you eat such exotic delicious food at home as well? What is your most favourite dish (can be from home or a restaurant)?

No, not at all. I eat very simple food at home, even in hotels. My family favourite dish is khichdi. The mushroom risotto is a personal favourite.

To remain healthy, do you exercise or follow a particular diet?

I do not.

Can you provide a simple recepie that you like to eat?

Here is an easy recipe for when you have guests at home, and no time in hand.

PANKO CRUSTED BHARWAN MIRCH, GOAT CHEESE MOUSSE, CHILLI AAM PAPAD CHUTNEY

Ingredients

Green chillies	2
Goat cheese	60 g

ourtsey: Manish Mehrotra

Red capsicum	5 g (diced)
Yellow capsicum	5 g (diced)
Roasted cumin powder	3 g
White pepper powder	2 g
Besan	30 g
Ajwain	1 g
Red chilli powder	2 g
Turmeric	1 g
Panko breadcrumbs	for crumbing
Oil	for frying
Sweet chilli sauce	30 ml
Aam papad	20 g (chopped)

Method

1. Cut the green chillies lengthwise from the centre.
2. Boil water and blanch the chilies.
3. Drain and cool.
4. Prepare the goat cheese mixture by adding small dices of red and yellow capsicum, roasted cumin and white pepper powder.
5. Stuff the green chilli halves with the goat cheese mixture.
6. Prepare the batter with besan, ajwain, red chilli and turmeric.
7. Dip the stuffed green chili in this batter and roll in the panko breadcrumbs.
8. Deep fry the crumbed chilies till the color of breadcrumb is golden brown.
9. Mix the chopped aam papad and sweet chilli sauce.
10. Serve the fried chillies with this sauce.

Recipe courtesy: Indian Accent, New Delhi
(Indian Accent Is An Old World Hospitality Concept)

MONISH GUJRAL Chef/Restaurateur/Author

Your grandfather invented the tandoori chicken as well as the butter chicken, two of the most iconic Indian dishes. What's the story to that?

It was in the early 1920s in Peshawar (in undivided India) that my grandfather invented the tandoori chicken. His mentor, who was sick, wanted to eat some light chicken dish. Those days the tandoors were used for baking nans and rotis only and the meats were eaten as kormas, pit-roasted kebabs. He thought of a novel idea to marinate the chicken with yoghurt and some mild spices and lowered it into the tandoor—what came out was the legendary "Tandoori Chicken". The dish became an instant hit once it was introduced in Moti Mahal in Peshawar. Later, he invented the butter gravy as he saw the tandoori chicken and tikkas became dry later in the day due to the heat of the tandoor. To be able to serve them and not waste them, he thought of a sauce which would make them soft and succulent. It was then when he invented the rich tomato-based butter-filled sauce and the "Butter Chicken" was born. Not only did the chicken see its new avatar but the humble black dal also was reborn as the "Dal Makhani" of the modern world.

As you travel abroad frequently, I'm sure you have tasted the different versions of butter chicken around the world. What is the situation of butter chicken abroad; and please comment on the authenticity compared to the original version.

Whenever I travel abroad and we are invited by fellow Indians to their homes, they always cook Indian food, especially dal makhani and butter chicken. Although the taste is good but I invariably hear from them that "it may not be able to compete with Moti Mahal standards but hope you enjoyed". Moti Mahal has set a hallmark for the butter chickens, the tandoori chickens and the dal makhanis around the globe.

Courtsey: Monish Gujral

What is your favourite cuisine and dish?

Like all hardcore Punjabis I love my tandoori. My favourite dish from Moti Mahal—dal makhani with khasta roti. Whenever I return from foreign trips, the first thing that I want to eat is the dal and naan or khasta roti. With every morsel, besides thanking God for the daily bread I do also thank my granddad for the daily dal and the humble roti.

Your job must require you to taste and create a lot of fattening food. How do you manage to stay fit despite this?

As a chef I have to cook and taste fancy food as a routine. Besides being a foodie and my love for cooking as well as eating good food one has to be careful as to what to eat and when to eat. "Like to eat and have to eat" does not mean that we risk our health. I believe in a healthy body and healthy mind. For being healthy I follow a strict exercise routine. I go to the gym every morning and train rigorously for more than an hour. In the evenings, if I come home early I do go for a jog. Another thing that I religiously follow is that I eat my dinner very early—around 7.30 pm—and avoid carbs at night and of course desserts. Drinking green tea during meals and avoiding cold water is also a good practice.

Are you more of a dessert or savoury person? What is your favourite dessert?

I am a dessert person, although I enjoy savouries as well. My favourite dessert besides the American cheesecake is the *gajar ka halwa* which my mom makes.

It's a known fact that butter chicken is a decadent dish in terms of its calorie content. Is it possible to make it healthier or low fat without compromising much on taste?

I always say that when you want to eat butter chicken just eat it and sweat it out later on the jogging machine or for kids in the soccer field. However, a low-fat version can be made with skimmed milk instead of cream and smaller portion of butter but that will be a compromise.

Could you please provide an easy recipe that you love?

I love white burfi with dates. Don't get me wrong. Date as in the date we eat, not what we go for. So here we go on a date with burfi!

DATES BURFI

Ingredients

Khoya	500 g
Castor sugar	½ cup
Cardamom poser	½ tsp
Dates pitted	1 cup

Method

1. Take a heavy-bottomed pan and keep on heat.
2. Add scrambled khoya.
3. Stir continuously till it becomes like a smooth dough.
4. Remove from heat.
5. Bring it to room temperature.
6. Add sugar, cardamom and dates.
7. Mix well.
8. Spread in a dish with edges.
9. Let it cool.
10. Cut into diamond shape and serve.

SARANSH GOILA Chef

During your childhood, what was your favourite food?

I am a dessert lover, from the very start. Having loads of jalebis and gulab jamuns in one go, those are fond memories for me. Apart from that I used to love paranthas of all sorts with extra filling in them.

How and when did your interest in cooking begin?

I started cooking when I was 12 years old. I was extremely passionate about cooking after I saw my grandfather cook dum aloo every Sunday. The first dish I ever really cooked was aloo parathas for 15 odd people on a late mehendi night at a family wedding. Where every spice was added by me and I guided my uncle to cook it. After that night, I started experimenting every weekend. I would make different dishes that I learnt from Chef Sanjeev's show and so, as a kid, I became very popular in my family as the "boy" who cooks.

You travelled 20,000 km throughout India to discover its food. What made you do this?

We came up with this idea to cover India in a way that hadn't been done before. Earlier, the plan was just to have a cameraman and a producer travel across India and document some rustic food stories. Not dhabas or hotels but food stories. Like, Rohtang pass has a 6-hour traffic jam every day, on the way to Leh-Ladakh. The jam is popular because it happens every day. You have to get stuck there as it is a part of the experience. There's this guy who waits for this jam to happen every day so he can sell his chaat. He does a 6km-trek, up and down every day, with his moving kitchen on his shoulders. It is amazing. He sells hundred portions of chaat every day, during a traffic jam. You see, such stories. That's what makes India and its food culture so brilliant and we wanted to bring this aspect

Courtsey: Saransh Goila

of our cuisine out. We were particular about the fact that it had to be a continuous journey—travel across India in one go. It's easy to catch a flight and go to another city. But if you travel by road, from point A to point B to point C to point D, on a continuous trip, that's when the journey is complete and you've soaked in the beauty of every city. So it was a very romantic travel idea, almost like a Motorcycle Diary-ish journey by a chef.

What is your favourite cuisine to cook?

It has to be Indian cuisine, not just because I specialise in it but because it is so diverse. With every 100 km, the food we eat changes—the flavour, colour, produce, basically everything. So, it never stops to amaze me.

Are you a fan of fast food?

In all honesty, I used to be a fan until I left college and realised that my eating habits were just doomed. I used to weigh 93 kg and I desperately wanted to be fitter and healthier. So I gave up fast food for a long while. So, no, I am not a fan of fast food and I do everything in my power to guide people to not be addicted to it as well.

What is your ultimate, most favourite dish to eat?

I love to eat what my mom cooks for me. Especially her Sindhi kadhi with matar pulao and aloo tuk is my all-time favourite.

Do you work out? If yes, then what is your regime?

Yes, I do. I run for 45 minutes every alternate day. I believe persistence is the key to losing weight. The challenge was to reduce the stubborn belly fat, tone muscles and saggy skin, the usual by products of initial weight-loss. I'm usually found on a cross trainer. People say a cross trainer is inferior to real running. That's a myth! The elliptic movement forces your calves, quads, biceps, triceps and even your core to work more. I cross train for 20–30 minutes at a moderate speed and I surely burn at least 200 calories.

It is a known fact that white sugar is a killer when it comes to health. What do you think is a good alternative to it in baking?

A lot of people will ask you to keep off sugar for a healthier life. But if you're a sugar lover like me, you know that the option isn't real enough. So, what do we do? Find sugar alternatives. Honey and jaggery are the easiest substitutes for sugar and also lend a new appeal to any drink or dish. If you want to take it a step further, use dates, especially for milk-based desserts. Make a puree of dates and you can add them to kheer, kulfi and rasmalai to indulge your sweet tooth, while cutting down on calories. For those afternoon or evening hunger pangs, keep a jar of almonds soaked in honey ready. It's the perfect recipe for instant dessert.

Lastly, could you please provide an easy, healthy recipe that you love to eat?

Definitely.

I've a very simple motto "Healthy food shouldn't taste like cardboard". So the ultimate challenge is to meet health halfway, where the dish can't be classified as unhealthy and it still tastes the same.

BROWN RICE BIRYANI

Well, I tried my hand at preparing a biryani with brown rice and, much to my surprise, it came out better than anticipated. The grains of brown rice anyway stand separate after cooking and have a bit to them, so that works in the favour of using them for a biryani.

Ingredients:

For chicken

400 g chicken, cut into pieces
3 cups mixed vegetables diced, (cauliflower, carrots, french beans)
2 tbsp garlic and ginger, chopped
4 onions, sliced

2 tbsp fried onion
½ cup yoghurt
½ cup chicken stock
60 g mixed dry fruit
1 tbsp garam masala (homemade)
¼ tsp turmeric powder
2 tsp cumin powder
1 tsp chilli powder
2 tbsp creen chillies
Mint leaves, a small bunch
Coriander leaves, a small bunch
1 tsp green cardamom
1-inch cinnamon sticks
2 bay leaves
1 tsp white pepper
Salt to taste
4 tbsp olive oil.

For rice
1 tsp rose water
2 tsp ghee
200 g brown rice
2 pinches saffron
3 tbsp fried onion
Mint leaves, a small bunch
Coriander leaves, a small bunch
1 tsp green cardamom
1-inch cinnamon sticks
2 bay leaves
2 tsp shahi jeera

Courtsey: Saransh Goila

Method

1. Marinate the chicken with cumin, turmeric, chilli powder, green chilli, garam masala, fried onion, salt and pepper. Keep this aside for 2 hours.
2. Heat a pan. Heat oil in it and add cardamom, bay leaf, cinnamon.
3. When it begins to crackle, add onion. Sauté till onion turns brown. Add ginger and garlic.
4. Add the marinated chicken and sauté till sealed. Add vegetables, dry fruits and chicken stock and cook for 15 minutes. Switch the gas. Top it with coriander and mint leaves.
5. Cook soaked and drained brown rice separately with cardamom, bay leaf, cinnamon, shahi jeera in salted water. Cook till it's 50% done.
6. Now take a heavy bottomed pan with a heavy lid. First add all of the cooked chicken which is almost cooked at the bottom. Top it with the cooked rice.
7. Dilute some saffron in 2 spoons of milk or water. Add this and rose water on top of the rice. Cover this rice with brown onions, coriander and mint. Cook it on slow fire with the lid tightly closed for 15 minutes. Let the biryani cook in its own steam.
8. Serve with papad, raita and pickle.

TIRATH SINGH Chef, Whole Foods/Ultra Cyclist

How did your passion for cooking begin?

My passion for cooking began as a kid of about 11 or 12 when I would bake cakes and cookies at home. I was very interested in the whole process of mixing a cake/cookie batter and then seeing it bake, and of course eat it.

What is your favourite dish to eat (home or restaurant)?

Very difficult to say, food is so varied and to make a single choice is just not possible, so I guess it will depend on a particular time and mood. Some of my favourites would be—mutton biryani, galouti kebab, really dark chocolate in any form, bhindi, yellow dal, methi aloo, medium-done steak, fish in virtually all kind of preparations.

Is fitness something you were always interested in? What made you interested in health foods?

Yes, I have always been interested in fitness. As a kid I would run and cycle, and now for the last 8–9 odd years I have been cycling exclusively. My interest in health foods or rather healthy eating would stem from the fact that once you get really interested in a sport and start progressing then you look at all options of improvement and one's diet is very important.

Since you are an ultra-cyclist, cycling over 25,000 km, what kind of a special diet do you follow?

I start my day with 20–25 ml of extra virgin coconut oil (raw), followed by a breakfast of 3 eggs and veggies. Lunch is a full meal with dal, veggies, chicken (or any other meat if at all), rice and yoghurt. Dinner is the same as lunch minus the carbs. In the evening, between meals, I have vegetable juice. I have made a choice to make my diet gluten-free and I

Courtsey: Tirath Singh

am much better off and have lost most of my belly fat. On my bigger rides I carry enough electrolytes (lemon with black salt and green tea, etc.), my "endurance bar" which I make at Whole Foods, and bananas. I try to consume at least 300 calories per hour while riding (not easy).

Due to lack of time or sheer laziness, a majority of the youth is consuming fast food. Any trick to stay away?

Education about food and nutrition! But really it is about making an effort and committing to better your lot. I mean what is the trick to stay away from smoking?

A major problem I faced was finding a good substitute for sugar in baking. Can you please recommend one? Also, what are some healthy fats that can be used in baking?

Use this new sugar called Diabliss. It is regular sugar treated with herbal extracts to bring the glycaemic index down to 45, which is brilliant! Alternatively, you can use dates, chopped raisins, chopped apricots, jaggery, palm jaggery (super sweet). Stevia is a good natural sugar substitute but can't replicate the properties of sugar, only the sweetness. Healthy fats like butter, ghee and all cold-pressed oils can be used in baking. Never use margarine and other hydrogenated fats. Don't skimp on the quantity of fats required in a recipe. However, moderation while consuming the product is important.

Since you are a chef with the biggest organic food organisation in India, and a sportsperson too, do you advice one should consume any of the protein supplements now so easily available in the market?

Eat natural. The market is full of all kinds of nonsense. Educate yourself about the various wonderful sources of proteins that are available in the world.

What's the best pre- and post-workout snack/meal?

My pre-ride meal/snack includes raw coconut oil and post ride I have a full breakfast—coffee, eggs and veggies. But really, eat whatever works for you.

Can you please provide an easy/ quick to toss up and healthy recipe that you really like to eat?

CHERMOULA FISH

Ingredients

Fish fillet of your choice

Marinade

½ cup parsley
½ cup coriander
1 tbsp roasted cumin powder
2–3 green chilli
salt to taste
3 tbsp olive oil
3–4 cloves of garlic
juice of 1 lemon

Method

1. Put all the marinade ingredients in a food processor and make a paste.
2. Take a fish fillet and apply this marinade generously and keep aside.
3. Grill the fish and serve with chargrilled veggies and carbs of your choice (polenta cakes go very well with this fish).

VIKAS KHANNA Michelin Star Chef

How did your passion for cooking begin?

I used to spend a lot of time with my grandmother as she cooked meals for the whole family. Simple jobs like shelling peas and making dough gave me immense satisfaction and strength. Even rolling breads at the Golden Temple gave me the power to feel that I can accomplish a lot in life.

Growing up, what was your favourite food?

Simple home-cooked meals like lentils, chickpeas, rotis.

Being a foodie with a knack for cooking, a major problem for me is to stay away from the stuff I make. How do you stay so fit despite all the culinary temptations?

It's really a problem trying to stay away from not eating everything that is cooked in my restaurant. But I think that training your mind is very important.

What is your favourite cuisine and dish to eat?

My favourite cuisine is Bhutanese, Nepalese, Tibetan and I love simple Indian homemade meals (anything).

Is fitness something you were always interested in? What's the secret to those 6-pack abs?

I don't smoke, drink and lead a very disciplined life.

Courtsey: Monish Gujral

How often do you have cheat days? And what would your ultimate cheat meal consist of?

Many times, especially when I am with my nieces. When we bake cakes, we eat them all. That is the only time I am cheating too much with sweets.

Typically what foods do you consume daily to remain fit? What do you usually snack on when you feel hungry?

I am a big Granola-Quinoa-Smoothie-Yoghurt-Egg White-Multigrain type of guy. I always keep granola bar and fruits with me, always.

Acknowledgements

My heartiest thanks goes out to Navroze D Dhondy, Sushma Bahl, Archana Sapra, Sumit Kapoor, Shobit Arya, Punya Vij, Indu and Vikram Kapahi, Natasha Kapahi, Ritie and Kunal Goswami, Harish Kotian, Ravi Dhingra, Charu Narain, Dr Rachna Singh, Prabha Agarwal, Gautam Kaul, Himanshu Chawla, Nin Taneja, Suraksha and Yogesh Gajwani and of course dad, Gautam Bahri, who is always ready to eat with me and my biggest critic! A big shout goes to Ishi Khosla, thank you Ma'am for your kind words, Chef Davinder and Chef Anuj at Hotel Le Meridien for so painstakingly going through all my recipes and all the "inspirational" gurus and celebrities who did not blink an eyelid before replying to all my mails.

Dada, Dadi, Nana and Nani—hope you are proud of me and know now why I've not been meeting you enough! Now we will have time to savour all these delicacies together.

Biggest thanks to my mum, Puja Bahri, for being the catalyst and getting me started. For cooking with me, trying out my recipes, editing, arguing, discussing, sampling, and being very patient about the fact that I decide to do this book during my final year in school! This book wouldn't have been possible without your invaluable inputs and the beautiful photographs that you took of my food—always ready with your camera, anytime of the day or night. Hope this book makes you proud...very proud!

Thank you NIYOGI BOOKS for having faith in me and agreeing to publish this book.

Shopping List

Cooking your own quick and healthy meals can be very painful if you don't have the right ingredients available. I always suggest and advice to stock up the pantry at least once a week. A well-stocked pantry is the best way to ensure you'll have everything you need to cook once you get home. Here is a list of the MUST HAVE ingredients that can be creatively used to cook up a storm in your kitchen! All these items are easily available online or at all supermarkets.

Spices and condiments

- Extra-virgin olive oil for salad dressings.
- Cold-pressed coconut oil for cooking and baking (preferably organic).
- Sesame oil for salad dressing and quick tossed vegetables
- Butter
- Organic apple cider vinegar (make sure it's with the "Mother" which is actually the sediments in the bottom)
- Balsamic vinegar
- Soy sauce
- Fish sauce
- Chilli garlic sauce
- Thai sweet chilli dip
- Sesame seeds
- Low-fat mayonnaise
- Wholegrain mustard
- Ketchup
- Barbecue sauce
- Crunchy peanut butter

- Tahini
- Gherkins
- Pitted olives
- Coarse sea salt
- Black peppercorns
- Onion powder
- Garlic powder
- Dried herbs: dried thyme leaves, oregano, mixed Italian herbs.
- Spices: chili powder, cinnamon sticks, ground cinnamon, coriander seeds, cumin seeds, dry mustard, paprika, cayenne pepper, crushed red pepper, turmeric
- Brown sugar
- Raw Honey
- Vanilla pods
- Pure maple syrup
- Unsweetened cocoa powder

Grains and Legumes

- Wholewheat flour
- Assorted wholewheat pastas
- Brown rice and instant brown rice
- Quick oats
- Couscous
- Quinoa
- Plain dry breadcrumbs
- Panko crumbs
- Chia seeds
- Amaranth flour

Nuts and Dry Fruits

- Walnuts
- Almonds

- Dry-roasted unsalted peanuts
- Assorted dried fruits, such as apricots, prunes, cherries, cranberries, raspberries, blueberries, dates, figs and raisins

Dairy Products

- Almond milk
- Coconut milk
- Coconut cream
- Low-fat plain yoghurt/vanilla yoghurt
- Low-fat vanilla ice cream or frozen yoghurt for dessert
- Good-quality parmesan cheese
- Sharp cheddar cheese
- Ricotta cheese
- Blue cheese
- Feta cheese
- Bocconcini
- Quark
- Mascarpone
- Tofu

Meat, Fish and Poultry

- Eggs
- Boneless and with bone chicken breast
- Smoked chicken
- Bacon
- Fish fillet (just any white fish)
- Medium-sized prawn

Table of Measures

The easiest and most convenient way to cook and bake is to use the standard US cups and spoons for measuring out ingredients, as different ingredients have different weights according to the difference in their volumes. For example, 1 cup all-purpose flour is 130 g, but 1 cup castor sugar will be 200 g. Although baking is about precision and accuracy, my recipes don't require precision. I have tried to keep it as simple as possible, as it makes things quicker and easier. All recipes in this book have the scope of adding or subtracting some ingredient here and there. However, to answer the call of duty of an author, I have compiled below a chart that provides Metric and Imperial liquid and weight measure equivalents of the US cups and spoons system.

US Cups and Spoons Measures	**Metric Liquid Measures**	**Imperial Liquid Measures**	**Metric Weights**	**Imperial Weights**
1 tsp	4.9 ml	0.1 fl oz	4.9 g	0.1 oz
1 tbsp	14.7 ml	0.5 fl oz	14.7 g	0.5 oz
1/4 cup	60 ml	2.1 fl oz	59 g	2.1 oz
1/3 cup	80 ml	2.8 fl oz	78 g	2.7 oz
1/2 cup	120 ml	4.2 fl oz	118.2 g	4.1 oz
2/3 cup	160 ml	5.6 fl oz	156.1 g	5.5 oz
3/4 cup	180 ml	6.3 fl oz	177.4 g	6.2 oz
1 cup	240 ml	8.4 fl oz	236.5 g	8.3 oz

ml-millilitre
fl oz-fluid ounce
g-gram
oz-ounce

Index